How to Propose Without Screwing it Up:

50 Common Mistakes Other Men Make and How to Avoid Them

License Notes

This book is licensed for your personal enjoyment only. This book may not be re-sold or given away to other people. If you would like to share this book with another person, please purchase an additional copy for each recipient. If you're reading this book and did not purchase it, or it was not purchased for your use only, then please purchase your own copy. Your support and respect for the property of this author is appreciated.

YOUR FREE GIFT

I'd like to reward you with FREE access to my popular podcast "The Art of Marriage Proposals" and two FREE bonus gifts ("25 Creative Proposals" and "25 Proposal Speech Templates") sure to help you nail two very important aspects of your proposal.

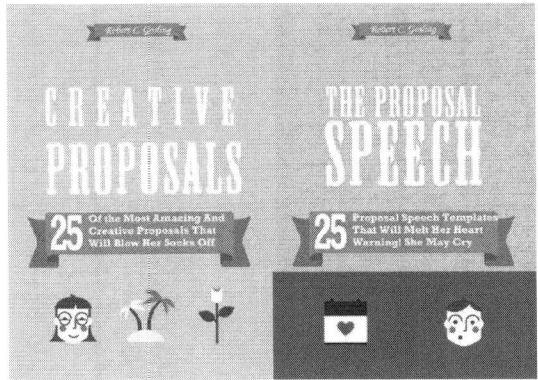

In the short and information packed podcasts, you'll hear from various experts, like proposal planners, ring specialists and men and women, just like you, on how to deliver a flawless marriage proposal.

Get free instant access to the fool-proof podcast and the special FREE bonus today.

To start listening and claim your prize, email wowproposals@gmail.com

Disclaimer:
Copyright © 2013, All Rights Reserved

No part of this publication may be reproduced, transmitted, transcribed, stored in a retrieval system, or translated into any language, in any form, by any means, without the written permission of the author. Understand that the information contained in this book is an opinion, and should be used for personal entertainment purposes only. You are responsible for your own behavior, and this book is not to be considered medical, legal, or personal advice. Nor is this book to be understood as putting forth any guarantee. The programs and information expressed within this book are not professional advice, but rather represent the author's opinions and are solely for informational and educational purposes. The author is not responsible in any manner whatsoever for any injury or result that may occur through following the programs and opinions expressed herein. All information within this book is presented for informational purposes only and may not be appropriate for all individuals.

Contents

Introduction

Section 1 - Ruining The Surprise
1. Chatter Box
2. The Reveal
3. Slippery When Sloppy

Section II - Basic Expectations
4. Taking a Stand
5. Cutting to the Chase
6. Uhh...Umm
7. Not Seeking Help
8. Whose Proposal Is it Anyway?
9. No Assembly Required
10. Say What?

Section III- Reaping What You Sow
11. Show Your Spirit
12. Father Knows Best
13. Don't be Cheap
14. There's No I in YES
15. Don't Steal her Limelight
16. The Joke's On You
17. From Left Field

Section IV- Organization
18. Public or Private
19. Getting Too Elaborate
20. Relying on The Unreliable
21. Proposing on a Holiday
22. Beauty and the Beast
23. Super Sketchy
24. Getting in Over Your Head
25. Majoring In The Minor

Section V - The Ring Thing
    26. Dude, Where's My Ring?
    27. Size Matters
    28. Getting it All Wrong
    29. Ring Flubs
    30. For Her Finger Only

Section VI - Nailing The Proposal
    31. Go Big or Go Home
    32. Timing is Everything
    33. The Goldilocks Effect
    34. Strike While the Iron is Hot
    35. Is There an Echo in Here?
    36. Liquid Courage
    37. Worst Places to Propose
    38. The Interweb
    39. Why So Serious?

Section VII - No Regrets
    40. Wrong Intentions
    41. Ready or Not
    42. The Guessing Game
    43. Making Assumptions
    44. Missing The Moment
    45. The Wrong Answer
    46. $#!t or Get Off the Pot
    47. Cry Me a River

Section VIII - Closing Statements
    48. Don't Sprint A Marathon
    49. It's Not Over
    50. Have a Back Up Plan

Introduction

From the outside looking in, proposing appears to be a simple and fairly straightforward process. There are no hard and fast rules, and every couple is unique, right? Wrong. There are indeed expectations and rules to pulling off a flawless engagement and most couples are more alike than dissimilar in the grand scheme of things.

The opportunity to make blunders is a very real and unfortunately, common reality. So much so, that a simple internet search will reveal hordes of message boards filled with women complaining about how let down they were with their guy's lack of romantic forethought and subsequently searching for some way to get over their disappointment.

Sadly, they probably never will. There are no do-overs when it comes to proposing to your girlfriend, so if you don't get it right the first time, be prepared to have a wife who will always associate negative thoughts with the way you proposed. There will be no special moment to reflect on when times get hard, just a nagging thought that you didn't care enough even then, and persistent doubts about your relationship.

I don't know about you, but if you aren't interested in doing everything you can within your means, to make sure your woman is not only satisfied, but blown away and secure in your love for her, by delivering a marriage proposal that she wants to tell everyone within earshot about it, then maybe the time isn't right or she's not the one.

However, the mere fact that you have invested in this book to make sure you get every aspect right, tells me that you have probably found true love.

I'm optimistic that you're right!

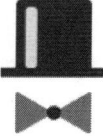   

Section 1 - Ruining The Surprise

1. Chatter Box

So, you've come to the life altering decision to propose to your girlfriend. Congratulations! Finding someone who you think you might want to spend the rest of your life with is no easy task, and provided all goes well, which I'm here to ensure, this will be one of the best days of your entire life.

Naturally, once you've felt the urge to propose to your girlfriend, the first thing you might want to do is ask your closest friends and family member for their advice, whether it be how to do it, where and when to do it, or if they agree with your decision at all. You might want to get as many opinions on the matter as possible so as to get different perspectives and multiple options to consider. However, the fact that you are thinking about proposing should be a closely guarded secret, that only a select group of people should be privy to.

Why is this so? Simply put, most people are terribly bad at keeping such exciting and wonderful news to themselves. If you notice, the above sentence mentioned people and not specifically any specific gender. That's because despite what the media may claim, men are just as big on gossiping as women are perceived to be. Not only should you be wary of spilling the beans to your female friends, but your male friends should also be chosen wisely.

You see, you might just think you're telling your best friend, but your best friend might share the news with his girlfriend in confidence, who then turns around and tells another individual. Before you know it, the news somehow reaches someone who will either let it slip, or be pressured into revealing his or her knowledge to your intended. Some people are easier to crack than others and won't take as much prodding before caving in. This is particularly rampant for couples who share groups of the same friends.

Although you may have spoken to your girlfriend about marriage in the past, or she may have a hunch that you are seriously thinking about popping the question, getting validation from an outside source that you indeed are going to make the commitment to her destroys the genuine shock and awe of her getting a proposal when she least expects it.

The same rule applies for telling or asking her friends for advice. First, they probably won't be able to give you any special information or insight that you can't get on your own, especially if you know your beau well. Second, even if you make them promise a thousand times over not to tell your intended, you are setting yourself up for the high likelihood that your surprise will be completely ruined.

2. The Reveal

Another mistake guys make is telling so many people beforehand, that once they finally get engaged and she goes to spread the word, she realizes that everyone already knows down to the finest detail. This is a classic mistake known as ruining the reveal.

A great part of being a newly engaged women is the novelty of being asked and telling as many people as she can, when and how the proposal happened. If you've given her a great story, she'll revel in giving the blow-by-blow detail of how it happened, what she was thinking, and even sharing any tidbits on the lengths you went to keep it a secret. Don't rob her of the joy of answering questions and retelling the story to others by beating her to the punch.

In writing this book, I interviewed a slew of men and women as well as drew upon the personal stories of friends and family members. One guy told the story of how he had made the rookie mistake of letting everyone know the exact date and how he planned on proposing to his girlfriend.

However, the day didn't pan out and he found himself faced with the decision to press on despite the moment not being right or holding off for the right conditions. He smartly chose to delay his proposal, but the following day his girlfriend was the recipient of tons of congratulatory phone calls and emails from friends and family who had been informed of his plan, on being an engaged woman. The morale of the story should be quite clear at this point.

Does this mean you can't ask for advice or confide in anyone? Absolutely not! Being smart and discerning is key. Treat everyone you know as though they were on a need to know basis. In other words, when it comes to deciding who should be in on the secret, the rule of thumb is to only tell those individuals who will be involved in implementing your proposal, your closest confidante who has demonstrated the ability to keep your secrets in the past, and/or has some valuable input that you won't be able to get elsewhere.

I'll talk about who those exceptional and lucky few people should be later on in the book, but for now, it's important that you bite your tongue and keep the news close to your chest. If you've already blabbed to everyone within earshot about your intentions, it may not be too late to salvage the damage.

It's a sneaky tactic, but if you fear you've made some questionable decisions in who to reveal your marriage proposal plans to, your best bet is to call everyone back up and tell them that you may have jumped the gun and that due to personal reasons you've decided to put proposing on the back burner for now. You don't have to expound on the personal reasons by making something sordid up. Keep it simple and if asked, say you'd rather not get into the details.

This maneuver might be a tad risky, since there is a chance your girlfriend has already been leaked the information from one of your gabbier friends. However, if she has yet to find out, the likelihood of the individuals you backtrack with telling her anything at all after the fact will be very low. Then, go on planning your proposal and feel free to explain later on to your very confused friends, that everything had worked itself out after all, when you call to break the news.

3. Slippery When Sloppy

It may seem a little strange but in this day and age where technology reigns this section has to be included and stated right off the bat. Do not, and I repeat, do not be sloppy and careless in the planning stage of your marriage proposal!

Hopefully, you've never needed to hide anything at all from your girlfriend in the past, which explains why you're not familiar with safeguarding and covering your online actions and interactions. That's great and all, but keeping your proposal from your girlfriend requires the finesse and paranoia of an expert two timing player. If you live together, or you have the keys to each other's apartments, it is especially critical that you heed this advice.

An innocent maneuver by her could result in her inadvertently finding out. Then, there are those women who suspect you may be up to something, and are able to find everything out without extensive detective work required due to your lack of internet savviness. I know some of you right now are thinking if she goes sleuthing she deserves to have the surprised ruined. However, I'll get to why even a girl who does a little checking up on her man may not entirely be at fault a little later on. It is your job to save her from herself or insecurities, which you could be lending to, and cover your tracks as much as mindfully as possible.

Don't worry, I've got you covered and have already thought of the most common mistakes men make when it comes to all things online related.

As previously mentioned, there are a few people I expect, and even encourage, you to correspond with in regard to helping you decide or orchestrate the proposal. The mode you use to get them up to speed must be carefully thought out though. Sending them a facebook message, e-mail, direct tweet, or text is an absolute no-no.

You should not be corresponding with the small list in your 'do tell' group via writing or anything that can be traced. Instead, have these important conversations face to face and/or on the phone or its equivalent (skype video or phone call), where there's no chance of someone you don't want overhearing your conversation. This will prevent you from having to password protect and lock everything, which may come across as you having trust issues.

Next, when doing research on anything marriage related, for example: ring comparison shopping on online jewelry stores, looking up the address of the nearby jewelry in town, marriage proposal ideas that worked or didn't (youtube.com has a great selection), reservations for her favorite restaurant, articles that tell you whether or not she's the one, message boards that lend support for guys about to propose, etc., be sure to close your tabs and completely quit each browser session.

It doesn't matter if you're doing all the research on your personal computer, laptop or ipad. You never know when she might need to use your device for an innocuous reason. Denying her access to your device, or asking her to hold on while you delete your history and close out your tabs will send alarm bells off in her head like crazy.

In fact, to save yourself from being vulnerable to the human tendency to make errors, your best bet would be to do all internet browsing through private or incognito browsing. I've never seen a browser that doesn't have this option, so don't worry if you're using Internet Explorer, Safari, Firefox, Google Chrome, or some other obscure browser you're likely to be the only one using. Again, don't rely on your memory to manually change to private browsing, because you will forget. To safeguard your browsing history, you are better off going into the settings of your browser and making private search an automatic function.

While you are at it, change the settings so that all of your cache and history is erased upon closing the browser. If you have safari, or another browser that culls and displays your top or most recent sites in your history, go through and delete all the pages you don't want your girlfriend to see lest she discover your secret plans, like perhaps the amazon page for this book. You will only have to do this once if you change your settings so that every session moving forward is under the privacy protection your browser provides.

This will prevent mishaps from occurring, like when your girlfriend goes to search for something completely unrelated on your laptop and is met with google's suggestions based on your previous searches or any pages that have to do with proposing that happen to start with the same letters.

While we're on this subject, forget about saving marriage proposal help websites in your favorites on your shared computer, but naming it under a title you think she won't open. The web address for the site will pop up in her search, despite what you name the site under in your favorites. If the web address has an obvious name, and most will since this lends to the website's search engine optimization and page rank, you will be vulnerable to the same outing I've been trying to prevent you from all along.

As for word documents or books, like the one you're reading, change the names of the file if it is obvious that the content is about your plans for becoming engaged. We've already done the legwork for you on this particular book, but other authors don't realize how huge a role discretion plays when naming their files and sending you e-mails.

By the way, I should stress that there's no need to get crafty and make up interesting book titles, since she may also find it interesting and want to read it. Work related names, a string of numbers or topics you are one hundred percent sure she has no interest in are probably the safest way to ensure she won't be tempted to sneak a peek.

It may seem like a lot of trouble to go through, but the reason for doing this is most word program editors and reader programs, like microsoft word and adobe reader, allow you to open files based on the last few recently opened works. If your girlfriend goes to open or save a document on your laptop and is met with "50 marriage proposal mistakes" in the open recent files, conveniently placed a mere mouse flick away from the open files link, she will instantly know what you're up to.

Again, you can change the settings of most software programs so that your recent files are never saved. To change the number of files that appear in the list in Microsoft Word, click the Microsoft Office Button > Word Options > Advanced. Under Display, in the Show this Number of Recent Documents list, click the number of files that you want to display and set it to 0.

To clear the list of files recently used, click the Microsoft Office Button > Word Options > Advanced. Under Display, in the Show this Number of Recent Documents List, click 0.

I recommend the first option of changing the number of files that appear in the list, because you will have to reset back to zero every time you use the program otherwise. Again, having a system in place that does not rely on your memory will ensure nothing falls between the cracks.

Strangely enough, Adobe does not provide an option to clear recently viewed files or limit the amount of files that show up on the list. Therefore, you'll have to use this workaround, which removes your access rights and stops the list getting created in the first place.

Open regedit > Navigate to "HKEY_CURRENT_USER\Software\Adobe\Adobe Acrobat\10.0\AVGeneral\cRecentFiles" > Delete any subkeys you find there to clear out old history > In the left pane, right click on "cRecentFiles" and select "Permissions" >
Click "Advanced" > Untick "Include inheritable permissions ..." and click "Add" when the dialog is displayed > Select the entry corresponding to your user name on the list and click "Remove" >
Click "OK" twice

Finally, for those of you with kindle e-readers, you can hide books you don't want anyone coming across relatively easily. There is no way to lock your kindle so that snoopers can't view all of your titles, but there is a way to tuck them so that they are just out of view when you are not reading. Use the rocker to select the title > scroll down to "remove from device" > Hit Select.

The kindle will put the books into the archive items folder, found at the very bottom of your listed books. You can't actually read books from the archived items folder, but you can restore them in under a second.

Open the list of archived items, select the book you want and it will download back on to the device and open back up to where you left off.

While it's not the worst thing in the world for her to find out that her proposal is shortly forthcoming, it does take away from the element of surprise. She might think she wants to know, but your job is to save her from her ignorance and make the experience all the more magic for her.

Section II - Basic Expectations

4. Taking a Stand

You know, I've always been a fan of the old saying, there's a place and time for everything. No adage could be truer than what we will discuss next, which is cardinal rule number three to not screwing up your proposal: Get down on one bended knee.

There is no exact clear historical origin of the idea of proposing with a bent knee, but the custom has been said to hearken back to the days of knighthood and chivalry when it was customary for a knight to dip his knee in a show of servitude to his mistress and his master. The knight would kneel before a tournament and wait for his lady to toss him her ribbon or colors, as an indication of her favor.

The gesture also bears a striking resemblance to many other ceremonial situations, including:

Royalty: Knights would kneel while being awarded honors from kings and queens, and still do to this day in most countries where Kings and Queens still rule the land. This can hold true for a proposal of marriage and can be seen as an honor.

Religion: Kneeling is appropriate during prayers and other religious ceremonies, including wedding vows for some faiths, such as the Roman Catholic Church and Protestants. Kneeling is also done to genuflect when entering a church or temple. When proposing, kneeling can have the same spiritual connotation and can be seen as a sign of respect.

Surrender: Bowing in supplication before a victorious enemy is typically seen as a gesture of surrender. When proposing, a couple commits to one another and the person kneeling surrenders oneself to being part of a couple.

Respect: The message behind the gesture can be that the man is offering himself wholeheartedly to the woman without reservations, elevating her to an exalted position in their relationship, and offering her the choice to determine the course of their relationship.

A more practical reason offered by engagementrings.com, is that a bent knee proposal puts the engagement ring in an elevated position between the couple, letting the light hit it clearly without being blocked by both individuals. This highlights the glitter of the ring as well as emphasizes the strength of the commitment.

Regardless of the origin, there is no more immediately recognizable romantic gesture than when a man proposes marriage down on one bent knee. It is highly symbolic and embodies the very essence of committing one's life to another.

The number of men that propose on one knee has diminished drastically over recent years, with some placing the blame on status, age, generation gaps or a swarming due to the feminine movements. Indeed, there are some women who identify as feminists who get offended by the act and would prefer not to be proposed to in this manner. However, they are outliers and make up a small percentage of women on a whole who will be disappointed if you choose to forego tradition.

A majority of women will appreciate the gesture of getting down on bended knee when asking for her hand in marriage, as such a seemingly insignificant gesture adds greatly to the seriousness and lovingness of the proposal. If you don't want to take my word for it, in an uncensored survey conducted by theknot.com, a huge community of women who gather to fawn over every wedding detail, nearly ninety percent of women said they "want their future grooms to put their kneecap to the ground as they ask the question".

Invariably, there will be someone reading this who will staunchly disagree with this rule, citing it as being too submissive or akin to begging for their taste. Perhaps looking at it from another perspective wouldn't hurt. There are really only a handful of moments in a woman's life that she fantasizes about that can be considered the hallmarks or milestones she'll never forget. They are her first kiss, deflowering, getting proposed to, getting married, and having children.

The evidence is staring you right in the face that failing to adhere to getting down on bended knee will more than likely leave your lady sorely disappointed and surely shatter a moment she has fantasized about for a very long time. You have to remember, even if you don't believe in it, if your girlfriend expects and desires you to do something so simple that will make her happy and pleased, why not oblige?

Which brings us back to the saying of "there's a place and a time for everything". The moment that you choose to propose is not the right place nor time to show your disdain for old traditions and take a stand on principle on a harmless gesture. Logic would state that if you are putting a ring on the finger, you've already decided that following the traditional path is something you are open to doing.

Since that's out of the way, let's dive into some ways I've heard and seen guys completely butcher this seemingly straightforward act.

To begin, please note, the expectation is to drop to one knee, not both. If you are going to give a speech, which I strongly suggest you do, you do not have to be on bended knee throughout your entire spiel. Speak your peace upright and then kneel down only when it comes time to ask the question and present the ring box.

Lastly, it should go without saying, that if you are asking in a manner that makes it completely impractical to propose on one knee or you have a physical disability, you can skip this rule. In every other instance, heed this advice.

5. Cutting to the Chase

Have you seen the YouTube videos or witnessed live proposals that resemble this scenario? A guy goes out of his way to come up with a really creative, Hollywood caliber proposal, and then catapults into asking his girlfriend those four magical words only to be met with a somewhat unenthusiastic yes. The proposal is over within the blink of an eye, no one is swooning and something feels off about the whole thing.

On the other hand, have you seen a modest proposal that wouldn't classify as being the most original or amazing spectacle, but the man delivers a really great, heartfelt speech, that by the end of it results in there not being a single dry eye in the crowd? Her emotion has been completely stirred up, she's bursting at the seams to say yes, passionately embraces and kisses him, and everyone just gets a feeling that they are one of the couples that will make it?

Here's the simple explanation—even the most unique marriage proposal will fall flat without a guy conveying why he has bothered to go through all the trouble in the first place. Giving some kind of marriage proposal speech at least shows your girl that you took the time to give it some thought and to put into words your emotions for her and the proposal. After all, most guys aren't typically known for being so vocal with those kinds of things, so saying something heartfelt and romantic really will make the moment extra special and memorable for her.

It's the difference between devouring a chocolate cake and savoring every scrumptious bite. Rushing cuts things short, and since we both know she's been waiting for this day a long time, anything that will enable her to luxuriate longer in the blissful experience you've created is a good thing.

Additionally, almost every romantic comedy, romantic drama, and even Disney movie ever made and watched by your girlfriend has set the precedence for what constitutes as a true display of love. It's not just the movies either, but young-adult and romance books are devoured every day, imprinting in her brain what she should be entitled to.

The grand speech that every guy inevitably makes in these overpriced chick flicks and books don't make it into every title by coincidence. The writers and movie industry executives have done a lot of research and observation to unlock the secret formula that gets women to part with their hard earned cash. What they know to be a fact is that women want to be taken on an emotional rollercoaster ride. It's why they enjoy a "good cry" and reading or watching things that will make them have strong visceral reactions.

You'll need at least a few meaningful words declaring your love and how much you want to marry her to compete on the level of those oversized recurring images and romanced filled novels she's been consuming since a tender age. Know that depriving her those words is as fulfilling as sex without foreplay for her, and sex with a happy ending for you. On the other hand, she will thrive on the promise of security your mere words provide.

Hopefully, you're noticing a running theme in the rules we've covered thus far; the great equalizer being going the extra mile to make it clear beyond the shadow of a doubt that you want to marry her.

Sure, technically you've proven that you want to marry her by buying a ring, setting up the perfect rouse to give her a genuine surprise, and getting down on one knee. That should say it all, but proposing is one of the few instances where your actions speak just as loudly as your words. Women want to be assured that you want to marry her for the right reasons and they can't seem to get enough verbal confirmation of your commitment and dedication to them.

If you want to be spared the unenthusiastic yes you're sure to get if you haven't said anything to speak to her emotions, which is mainly triggered by your words, have a speech memorized. Yes, memorized. You will be downright nervous when you propose, which will make it very difficult to think on your feet and say everything you want to say.

Reading your feelings from a piece of paper isn't the most romantic thing in the world and comes across as taking the easy way out. Stuttering your speech because you haven't properly committed it to memory won't be the least bit cute or flattering. You'll simply come across as unprepared and unsure of yourself. You want to be looking into her eyes and deliver a confident message so she knows its coming straight from your heart and a place of certainty.

Sounds like a lot of work? It's not really, but most men think it is and hope she won't notice if they just leave the whole proposal speech part out. Put it this way, you notice when your woman does or doesn't go the extra mile to please you, right?

Look, I get it, you're not a sappy kind of guy and writing smooth, romantic words doesn't come naturally to you or simply isn't your style. You don't have to be a modern day Casanova to nail this though. There are tools and professionals that can help make this process a thousand times less difficult than it appears to be.

You have two options at your disposal for preparing a speech: go it alone or hire someone to help. If you decide to go it alone, sit down and take some time to reflect on the message you want to convey. Some questions you might want to ask yourself for inspiration include:

> What did you think when you first met her?
> What traits and quirks do you love about her?
> What do you have now that you didn't before you met?
> What goals and values do you two share?
> When did you realize that you might want to spend your life with her?
> What about her inspires you?

Reflect on your relationship and answer these questions and more until you have included everything you want to say. One good tip to follow when crafting your speech, is to make your final words the more important ones, since chances are she'll be so giddy and taken back when she realizes what's going on, that she might not fully grasp what you're saying to her at first. You can also give her time to collect herself if you want to make sure she hangs on to every word.

Your speech need not drag on forever and it shouldn't be so short that she can blink and miss it entirely. About 60 to 120 seconds is plenty of time to melt her heart. This allows you to get a few amazing sentences in and her to remember and share it with friends and family. As soon as you start to speak, the adrenaline will start pumping and time will slow down for both of you.

A minute can feel like an hour, and that's why you don't need to worry about preparing a Shakespearean monologue. Besides, when you start to get into upwards of two minutes and beyond, you teeter on the fine line of losing her attention, boring her to tears, or making it all about your performance.

Email wowproposals@gmail.com to get a foolproof template for crafting your proposal speech on your own. You'll be able to see 25 of the most romantic marriage proposal speeches of all time, personalize the details to reflect your relationship and come out looking like a hero.

If you feel like the above might as well be telling you to learn Cantonese in a day, and you want to guarantee you'll knock this important component of your proposal out of the park there is another option. Luckily for you, there are people who have made a full time career in helping others get their words just right, for a very affordable price. These individuals are called professional speechwriters, and there are some who specialize in marriage proposal speeches.

A professional proposal speechwriter is a writer who is an expert in putting words together to succinctly and eloquently get your thoughts across. It's just like hiring a general speechwriter, but one who would make any romantic comedy writer pin his tail between his legs. You can always request the sap be turned down a notch, or ratcheted up to the max, although let me remind you that you're going to have to ultimately deliver the speech, so don't go overboard.

As it just so happens, I am an expert in this category and my company has assisted over 200 men polish up their proposal speech, wedding vows, and wedding toasts so that they sparkle even during an eclipse.

Getting a professional alleviates the extra work it takes to find the right way to say exactly what you want to say, and 60% of women remember the words their husbands said when they were proposed to so they'd better be good. Going this route also frees up time for you to focus on the million other tasks that need to get done. You'll see there are quite a few of them as you continue to read.

All you have to do is provide a few details, and my company does the rest. For a very affordable price, you receive a flawless speech, up to two-minutes, with unlimited revisions. If you for some reason want a longer speech, no problem. If this is something you are interested in and you want to learn more, email me with the subject "Write my speech" to get all the information about our service and prices.

6. Uhh…Umm

Once you have your speech all sorted out, you're well on your way to delivering the best proposal ever. Well, almost. As mentioned before, you'll need to practice and memorize the speech so that you can deliver it coherently in the high-pressure moment that is your proposal, when all eyes and ears will be on you.

This is especially important if you plan on making a very public display of your affection, and capturing the entire thing on video. You don't want to cringe every time your girlfriend or her friends and family want to see how the event unfolded in real time, or even worst, pay for a video that your girlfriend doesn't really want anyone else to see because you tanked.

Any professional public speaker will tell you that the reason most people fear public speaking, and suck so bad at it, is because they are not duly prepared.

For example, if you had to give a public speech that consisted of saying your name, where you reside, where you were born, your parents and siblings' names and the educational institutions you attended, you would have no problem! You know these things like the back of your hand—in fact, they are committed to your memory and you probably couldn't forget even if you wanted to. The second you start to flub is when you aren't so sure about the details because you either don't know or remember them. Well, the same applies to your speech.

There is no quicker way I can think of to destroy all the effort you've put in to getting everything else just right by blabbering or peppering every sentence with umms, uhhs and nervous eye darts as you try to recall what you are supposed to say. Commit it to memory until you know it just as well as your name, and performing under the spotlight won't leave you looking like an unprepared, blabbering basket case.

Some helpful tips for not forgetting your lines are:

Let your speech ring true

Tell your story. As I've already covered, remembering your lines get easier the more the things you need to remember are already embedded in your brain. A situation that you experienced has a natural sequence, which helps you recall events. The truth, which you've lived and breathed, will be super easy to recall as opposed to embellishments or someone else's truth.

If you are preparing your speech solo, make sure there is a natural progression or flow to your paragraphs. Generally, a professionally prepared speech should already contain this element (and if you go with my proposal speech writers, you can be assured of this fact).

Memorize the outline
Break the speech down into an outline using bullet points and memorize the outline before delving into the actual full paragraphs.

For each concept or bullet, take the key word and turn it upside down, enlarge it, color code it, change the font. Exaggeration makes the concept more memorable and aids retention

Read the speech slowly
As you read the speech aloud, do it slowly, hearing every word as you speak. Try to focus on the words and their meaning as you go on reading the speech until you understand every point perfectly. If the speech has been prepared by you reading it slowly two

to three times is going to help you in memorizing it. However, if the speech was written by someone else for you, this step will help you in getting yourself acquainted with the words you might not be inclined to normally use in the speech.

Record your Speech in your own voice
With the help of your free computer software, or a recording device, such as a voice recorder or your phone, record yourself reciting the speech in a clear and audible manner. Listen to it when you're on the way to work or the gym in your car or on the train. Try to speak along with the words when you are out of clear earshot of anyone you wouldn't want overhearing you.

Divide it into manageable chunks
Do yourself and favor and don't try to memorize your entire speech all at once. Break it up into manageable sections and work on one section at a time. Don't move on to the next section until you have mastered the previous one. Also, build on top of each section as you progress. For example, once you memorize paragraph two, be sure you can go back and recite paragraphs one and two in succession, without pausing, before moving on to paragraph three and beyond.

Try backwards memorization
If you are finding it annoyingly difficult to memorize your speech in top down order, try taking the backwards memorization approach. To begin, break

the speech up into short paragraphs. Next, pick the last paragraph instead of the first one while memorizing the speech and carry on learning until you reach the first paragraph.

Try the Loci Method
There are some who think using remote memory, memorization involving repeating things, is the only way to memorize something but that isn't true. Remote memory is how you probably learned your ABC's, multiplication table, and geography in school. An alternative method, that in some circles is considered the best way to go, is the loci method (pronounced "low-key").

As the story goes, a Greek poet named Simonides delivered a performance at a banquet hall. He was called away unexpectedly and shortly after he left, the entire building collapsed, killing everyone inside. Simonides helped identify the victims by using the image in his mind of various spectators watching him from the audience; in this way, he could picture where they were seated.

Utilize the loci method to reinforce the speech in your memory by making use of your imagination and start visualizing the words of your speech as you say them. This visualization of the words is going to reinforce your memory of the speech and will help you in recalling the words when you actually go to deliver it in front of your lady and an audience of spectators.

Write down the speech while listening to it
The more senses you can involve the better. This memorization tip requires you to write down the words of the speech while listening to it (preferably in your own voice). Writing has its own way of reinforcing the material and embedding it into your memory. Since you would be writing the speech while listening to it, both your senses of hearing and sight are going to absorb the information that goes into the brain.

7. Not Seeking Help

In every field there are professionals, experts, or gurus that have devoted themselves to mastering their subject. They're good, and they know it, so they place a price on helping those who haven't or don't want to put in the same amount of time to acquire the knowledge they have.

Such is the case with professional proposal planners. Never heard of them? You're not alone. Marriage proposal planning is a subset of event planning that focuses primarily on marriage proposals. A Men's Health survey found only 1% of their respondents had used a proposal planner to help with the big moment.

What exactly does a proposal planner do? Well, they do exactly what their title suggests—they help men plan creative and romantic proposal ideas that are tailored to their girlfriends, as well as help execute the idea to a tee. You can elect to just pay for a few personalized ideas separately from the execution, or just for them to execute an idea you already have.

Another part of their job description is to alleviate the stress that normally accompanies such an important day. If you can't come up with great original ideas to save your life, have the organization skills of a headless gnat, or have a very busy work life that demands a lot of your time and attention, do yourself a favor and hire a proposal planner to help you plan and execute for a flawless day.

The cost isn't completely out of reach for most men. Many proposal planners charge anywhere between $99 to $200 to give you two to three ideas tailored to you and your girlfriend's relationship background. How they accomplish this is by interviewing you to get to know your significant other, their likes and dislikes, and your budget. Based on the interview, they brainstorm and create personalized and unique ideas for your occasion.

Where you may need deeper pockets is if you want to use their services to actually carry out the idea. For example, you can leave the task of calling up companies, arranging details, purchasing all the romantic items (flowers, chocolate, champagne, etc.) to them, but you will pay dearly for this convenience.

Many guys are shelling out anywhere from $1000 up to $10,000 to impress their ladies with an out-of-this world proposal orchestrated by a proposal planner.

Before you shake your head in disgust, realize that the $10,000 price tag is often the result of airfare, hotel accommodations, and the like. Obviously the more outrageous the proposal and the more popular the proposal planner is, the higher the cost.

When choosing a planner, one question you should ask is how long they've been in business. Some proposal planners are simply failed wedding planners looking for a way to supplement their other business. Meanwhile, others have simply jumped aboard the proposal planning trend in hopes of squeezing a few thousands dollars from clueless guys.

There are no agencies regulating proposal planners, and you don't have to go to school or get any special training to get started in the business. There's no barrier to entry. Look at the planner's resume and track record, as the legitimate ones will have videos, YouTube channels, testimonial blogs full with pictures, and ideally, some press coverage. You could also ask to be connected to a few of the planner's clients to ask questions about their satisfaction. Any planner worth his or her salt shouldn't recoil at providing you with at least one reference.

Another alternative to proposal planners are concierge services. For example, The American Express Platinum Card Concierge service has consultants who help fulfill card member requests, anywhere in the world, 24-hours a day. They have reported noticing a trend for members who request help with marriage proposals.

Where a proposal planner or concierge consultant may come in handy is for the following:

A Family Affair
More men are surprising the bride-to-be by secretly organizing family and friends to be present at the time of the proposal. However, getting the family all together involves making phone calls, following up and getting them the details of what they should and shouldn't do on the day of so as not to blow your cover.

Depending on the size of your family, organizing such a task can be quite time consuming and frustrating. Ponying up the dough for a proposal planner to usher everyone to their place, give them instructions, and handle any complications may very well be worth it for such instances.

Destination Proposals
So, you want to propose in New York or Las Vegas, where you and your girlfriend happened to meet. Sweet, the only problem is you live in Europe.

Planning romantic, destination-based proposals with elaborately planned weekends filled with exciting activities can be very hard to do when you're half way across the country. Calling in a professional can make your life a heck of a lot easier, as well as the trip more enjoyable for you both in the long run.

One final alternative to getting professional help from a proposal planner to compensate for your total lack of romantic inclinations is going with a pre-planned proposal package. Some companies offer special marriage proposal packages that come with every detailed already planned out for you. For example, Princess Cruises offers a package that allows you to propose on any of their cruise ships via the big screen for movie screening night.

Princess will provide the videographer and put together your video package for you, so you just have to worry about escorting your lovely lady to the screening, presenting the ring and remembering your speech. For the entire duration of trip, you are also treated to massages, VIP treatment, and a beautiful suite, and of course you get to video as a keepsake.

Proposal packages are really great, but unless you thought of taking your girlfriend on a cruise, it would be difficult to find by simply typing it into your search engine.

Going it alone when you know you simply don't have the availability or propensity to carry out your proposal is a big mistake. Whether you choose to go for a proposal planner for the perfect idea, hire a concierge to coordinate all the details, or opt to purchase an all inclusive proposal package from a company, knowing when you need help and seeking it out will be one of the best things you can do if you want to pull off the perfect proposal.

If you worry that your girlfriend will think of your proposal as less romantic because you didn't plan every single detail or decorate the space, don't be. Most women will be impressed that you were willing to put your hard earned money into giving her the experience of a lifetime.

8. Whose Proposal Is It Anyway?

A big question you are going to find yourself facing at the beginning of the planning stage is what activity, event, and/or location you should choose that will resonate with and appeal to your girlfriend. You want something that she'll find cool, unique and interesting, right? Well, most guys say that's what they want, but somehow along the way end up planning a proposal that *they* think is cool as opposed to something she would love.

Take sporting event proposals, for example. I'll expound more later on why this is one of the worst places you can propose, but the majority of the men who propose at sporting events do so because it ties into their interest and passion, not hers. Even if she is a huge sports fan, this is one time she will want the day or evening to be all about her. Proposing at the game reeks of trying to kill two birds with one stone. No bueno.

If your aim is to deliver a perfect, story-book proposal that would make a harlequin writer proud and reader hot and bothered, your job is to think hard about the things that your girlfriend loves and remove yourself from the equation.

Start by asking yourself the following questions:

> Where has she always wanted to go?
> What has she always wanted to do?
> What are her hobbies?
> What would be different from the mundane?
> What's her favorite musician/artist?
> What have you been talking about doing forever?
> What has she been trying to get you to do forever?

Make a list and start looking into the options that are feasible, within your budget, and would apply to whether she wants a public or private proposal. If you can combine elements, do so. Don't be afraid to pack it in.

For example, if she has a personality that lends itself to a more public proposal, has wanted to learn how to tango for ages and tried to convince you to do it with her, you could surprise her with a tango dance lesson. Coordinate with the owners of the studio to have you both take the center stage towards the end of the class and play your favorite song in lieu of the tango music. Recite your speech and propose. Celebrate afterwards at a restaurant she has been dying to try with some close family and friends. Note, it would probably be a good idea to secretly take lessons without her so that you aren't stepping on her feet and leading her into a wall the night you propose.

If you notice in the example above, every thing that you have chosen to incorporate in your proposal is centered around your girlfriend: her desires, what fits her personality, what is important to her. Don't forget this day is about elevating her and making her feel super special, not about your desires, what fits your personality and what you have always wanted to do. If you get this right, you'll be golden. Ignore this rule at your own peril.

9. No Assembly Required

I get why a guy would want to ask his girlfriend questions about how she would want to be proposed to, but actually trying to sit down and get instructions from your girlfriend on where, how, and when to propose is one of the most unromantic and lame proposal mistakes you can ever make.

Trust me when I say, she'd much prefer that you come up with a plan, any plan, than ask for her input. This blunder is as bad as when you ask girl out on a date, show up to take her out, and then proceed to ask her what she wants to do. Show me a single girl on the planet who likes their man to be indecisive and put all of the work on them, and I'll show you a woman who is probably secretly a dude.

Don't get me wrong here, it is completely acceptable to have a sit down heart to heart chat to decide whether you are ready to marry, but the proposal itself should be exciting, romantic, and surprising. None of those elements are present when she is involved in the planning. The most you should try to gather from your girlfriend in regard to the proposal is whether or not she has an affinity for a public affair involving a large crowd and her friends and family, or an intimate affair involving just the two of you.

10. Say What?

Speaking of your proposal speech, just because you have one doesn't mean that you are in the clear. It is precisely what some men elect to say in their speech that puts the entire proposal into a tailspin. Sadly, it would appear some guys were just born without a romantic bone in their body, and as a result often suffer from foot in mouth syndrome.

Sticks and stones may break her bones, and your words can definitely hurt your girlfriend, so choose them wisely. Proposing is not the time to be a stand up comedian or funny guy, lest you run the risk of offending and embarrassing her and coming across as an insensitive jerk. It's the time to be the caring, sweet and charming guy.

Again take time to craft something heartfelt or hire a proposal speech planner, and as long as you stick to the script, you won't have to give a second thought to whether your words will offend your sweetheart. Writing a half-assed speech yourself without putting much thought into it, or ad libbing could potentially result in leaving you with a big problem in the form of a sulky, annoyed girlfriend or a flat out 'no'.

To give you a few ideas of what should absolutely not make its way into your grand speech, I've put together a list of some of the stupid remarks that have been made by men while proposing, below. Whatever you do, don't make the same unfortunate mistakes unless you want your girlfriend's blood to boil and strip away all the joy out of what should be one of the most memorable and happiest experiences of her life.

We're not getting any younger
Wow. Saying you're not getting any younger, or any other version of that sentence like, "It's probably time we settled down", and she'll hear loud and clear that you're settling. This statement is the equivalent of saying, you want to marry her solely because you don't think you'll be able to find anyone else better now that your hair is receding, you've put on some weight, and you're getting up in age.

Which woman in her right mind would be thrilled about being insulted by suggesting that the only reason you are proposing is because of the amount of time that has passed by, while simultaneously being told she's getting old and should settle for you in return? Even if you were contemplating using these words in jest, I'd recommend reconsidering since it's really nothing to joke about or funny.

I know this is what you want
When a man says, "I know this is what you want" when proposing, he is saying, "you twisted my arm and I'm finally going to cave to *your* wishes". There's no other clearer way of letting it be known that proposing wasn't your idea, and that it still isn't. If you, in fact, feel that you are asking against your own will or better judgment see rule #40 - Wrong Intentions and Rule #41 - Ready or Not.

We have to / It's the right thing to do
I touched on marrying because of other people's expectations and why it's a piss poor reason to get engaged before, so if you find yourself wanting to even utter these words or finding truth in them, you should probably start looking into the return policy on the ring.

Even worse than going through with the proposal realizing (or not realizing) your true shaky intentions, is voicing it to your girlfriend. When you cave to expectations to get married solely because you're about to have a baby, already have a child together, or you've been together an embarrassingly long time, you're not getting married on your own terms and of your own volition.

Nobody wants to hear that marrying them is a chore, a simple duty to be performed, or the only 'morally right' option. They want the marriage to be born out of an intense love and commitment.

The morale of the above examples is to take the moment seriously. Do not be sarcastic, or give the impression that you're settling or proposing against your good will or better judgment. Be cognizant of your words and the meanings behind them. Again, be sure to read my free book on some of the best proposal speeches for inspiration and do not deviate from a formula that works.

Finally, run your speech by someone you can trust to give you honest feedback on any area that might not sit well with your fiancé—a phrasing that can be misconstrued or a comment that doesn't add, but detracts, from your message of love and devotion. Women are usually better at catching these things so a sister, female cousin, or very close friends are good bets.

Section III- Reaping What You Sow

11. Show Your Spirit

I want to start off this section by defining a word that sums up everything I am about to say regarding the missing element of all too many proposals perfectly: En·thu·si·asm - en'THoōzē͵azəm/ *noun* - intense and eager enjoyment, interest, or approval.

Want a guaranteed way to sour your marriage proposal? Fail to show any enthusiasm for marriage and/or the moment and you'll be well on your way. Attitude accounts for everything, and it is definitely possible for a man to invest time and money planning a proposal, and then display in other subtle ways an attitude that doesn't quite match up to his actions.

It's important to note, some guys who screw up this rule may do so unwittingly. Perhaps their personality is to mask or shield their emotions, or get excitable about very few things. It's just they way they are, and their girlfriends have come to expect it. All the more reason to step it up during the proposal if you are this guy.

A woman used to a man like this will be bowled over if he displays emotion and excitement for proposing, because she'll know he only reserves that level of enthusiasm for very select few things.

On the other hand, a man who wears his emotions on his sleeve who fails to get excited about this particular event in his life, will definitely signal red flags to a woman.

This common mistake is regrettably committed by a lot of guys because they erroneously fail to realize its importance to a woman. That stuff about ignorance being bliss doesn't apply here. Know that your girlfriend will be watching you closely and deducting points from the proposal every time you mangle an element. To you, it may seem like she's looking for reasons to be let down, but to her she's looking for signs that you're the one she's meant to be with and that you're in it for the right reasons.

Luckily, I'm here to steer you on the right path, as it can be easily fixed and most guys will have the right intentions.

Who Do you Call?
Once you get to a yes, does not mean your proposal experience is over. It can immediately follow her

acceptance, after sharing a kiss and intimate moment with you, or the day after, but eventually she will want to let the important people in her life know that she is now an engaged woman.

Why? Besides the fact that women like to share, it's her way of saying that she's excited about being engaged to you and wants the world to know you want to make an honest woman out of her.

Can you imagine how you would feel if you proposed and she didn't want to tell a single soul? No Facebook status change, no ring photo posts (especially if she is active on social media normally), no screechy phone calls to her girlfriends. It wouldn't be very comforting right? In fact, you'd be down right alarmed and convinced you made a big mistake (your chances of getting that ring back is low).

Except, men do this to their women all the time. While she's busy calling everyone she knows, updating her status on Facebook and posting pictures on twitter, most guys make the big mistake of doing nothing and telling no one—leaving it all up to her to make a fuss.

Match her enthusiasm level by calling your parents, siblings and best friends, and taking a few seconds to update Facebook and wherever else you are currently sharing the important happenings in your life (e.g. - a blog, YouTube, etc.).

Having said all that, I should stress that it's very hard to fake or dial in enthusiasm successfully unless you're a classically trained actor. Most people can spot fake excitement or joy from a mile away, so if you aren't genuinely revved up about proposing to your girlfriend, abort and assess. Add to this the fact that most women know their men very well by the time he chooses to propose, and she'll be able to feel rather quickly whether something is off.

12. Father Knows Best

This may seem as outdated to some men as dropping down on one knee, but nine out of ten women want you to have sought her parents' permission before asking her to spend the rest of her life with you. That's 90% of women, or what you would call the overarching majority.

If that is the case, then where did this idea come from that guys don't have to or shouldn't go seeking the parents' blessing before asking for their daughter's hand in marriage? It's just a hunch, but I think perhaps it's a case of just the loudest women who shout it from the rooftops that they aren't their parents' property and don't need permission to marry, drowning out the silent majority.

It is your job to ask or to find out if this is important or offensive to her. I hate to generalize, but the only women who seem to get offended and angered by a man asking for his girlfriend's parents' advice, are feminists and very alpha type women.

If you're not familiar with the term alpha woman—it's usually only used to describe men—I'll break it down for you. An alpha woman is the dominant woman in a group. She is typically assertive, powerful, strong, confident, and a big earner. She likes to be on equal footing with men and doesn't want to be seen as a "weak" or "needy" woman. She's very independent, and thus the idea that you need to clear things with her father or parents does not appeal to her, as she interprets such actions being owned and needing clearance.

It is tradition to ask for a father or both parents' blessing, and remember you are not just marrying her you are marrying into a family. The father is considered the "covering" that the daughter is under. For that matter, it shows complete respect and honor for the man to ask first. Do not take that moment away from your future father in law as this might build a little resentment.

One thing is for sure, fathers (and mothers) won't get offended at being asked and many expect to be involved. Besides, it shows that a man is mature enough to do the respectful and right thing even if it's hard/scary to do, which is always a plus! It lets the woman know that her fiancée has thought this through and that the groom has her daddy's approval. Giving all parties confidence that this a well thought out and positive step in their lives.

> If you do not have the courage or respect to ask her parents permission this does not reflect well on how you see the relationship.
>
> If her father says no, which is unlikely if she's over the age of 21, ask her anyway. He cannot stop you, and you will be the better person for it.

If your girlfriend does not know her father or he has passed, you can ask her mother or the closest male figure in her life instead.

13. Don't be Cheap

I am happy to inform you that the vast majority of women are not money hungry or ruthless gold diggers only attracted to your earning potential. However, no woman is attracted to a cheap or frugal (same difference) man. In fact, being stingy is one of the most off putting characteristics in a man, according to women. The good news is that is less to do with money itself, and more to do with a mindset and what that represents.

Women tend to read between the lines of your actions and draw parallels between what you do today and how you will act tomorrow. How you spend your money is an indirect reflection of your spirit and personality.

A generous man will not only be generous with his wallet he will be generous with his time and with his feelings. For example, if you treat your girlfriend to a fancy meal, offer to pay for the taxi or show generosity towards friends, she will find this attractive. Therefore it is of the utmost importance to be generous with your time, feelings and savings during the proposal.

To be honest, it's more fun for both of you when you are generous. Consider going to a live concert versus listening to a band on your iPod. It just cannot compete. The same thing goes for a proposal. You have to go for the real deal.

By nature women are more generous to their men than vice versa. You may be scratching your head at that one, but if you think about all the stuff she does because she thinks it will make you happy (the money she spends on her looks—hair, makeup, workout classes, clothes, shoes, the things she does in bed that she doesn't particularly love, cooking, cleaning, picking up after you, planning things for you both to do, and the list goes on).

They are nurturing beings that are wired to take care of people and things. That's why it's more difficult and a chore for men to be generous. This is the perfect opportunity to fill and balance out the generosity account. The benefit is that women really do love to satisfy their men and she will recognize, repay, and reward your generosity.

By no means am I indicating that you should always pick up the tab and fork out the dough to cover all her expenses and every material desire. Your girlfriend shouldn't view you as a free ride or her meal ticket. However, this is an exceptional moment and should be treated as one. She shouldn't have to open her purse and come out of pocket even once during this day. Make it count; you only have one shot at this.

14. There's No I in YES

It is very important to plan the day around her. So think of her wants, needs, and schedule. I can't stress enough that the day you propose is not the time to be selfish. If you are going to be in a long term relationship, both of you will need to play the appropriate roles at the right time. This day will be about her, and if we're being real, so will the wedding day. But this woman will likely carry your children and give birth to them. So obviously when you think about it in context this is a very small price to pay.

There are three basic elements that you need to combine which I will go through in detail below. Each element is very important but it's the sum of all the elements that creates the synergy of a perfect proposal.

These are very basic pieces of the puzzle that you will have to assemble in order to impress her.

Her wants

These are points that she would like you cover. They are essential but carry less weight than her needs.

Originality is thought of as one of the key factors of a perfect marriage proposal but some men get carried away and focus on this way too much. See #16 Joke's On You, for more information and details on this matter.

Creativity is a lot safer than originality, this allows you to take a proven formula and put your own twist on it. A Big diamond will always impress a woman but its not who they will be marrying. Be sensible, purchase something in your price range. Refer to "Size matters"

Needs

These are factors that you must include in you proposal. The good news is that they are not expensive and are easy to follow as long as you are aware of them.

Acting considerate towards her and her needs is the most romantic thing you could possible do. If you act inconsiderate on the day or leading up to it she will be disappointed with you.

A thoughtful proposal is essential as this is an indicator that you have paid attention to the relationship and to her. This is no time to hold back, be generous but within reason, see "Don't be Cheap", for why this is so essential.

Schedule

This is her day to shine and she should be the center of attention. In other words you cannot steal the spotlight and more importantly you need to be sure no one else will take the spotlight from her in the coming days, see #15 - Don't steal her limelight.

Avoid planning a midweek proposal if she has a regular job. Similarly, if she is swamped with work or stressed out about a hobby (e.g. the marathon or planning an event for the organization she volunteers for), you might want to skip proposing until after everything has died down.

If she's about to go off traveling, and you won't see her for a few weeks, perhaps save the proposal until she comes back so that she doesn't spend the earliest days as an engaged woman solo.

The holidays, like Christmas and Valentine's Day are potential minefields. Scheduling the proposal around her calendar is a crucial element and is looked at more closely in the #21 - Proposing on a Holiday.

Making time to see family and friends after the fact also needs to be considered. Ideally you want to do it sooner than later while she's still on a high from the event.

Of course, in today's day and age many families are spread across the world. Even a country like the US can have a family split between east and west coast in different time zones. If this is the case it can be a good idea to propose in the lead up to, but not on one of the major holidays.

15. Don't Steal her Limelight

This is her day. She does not want to share it with anyone else or another monumental occasion. Repeat this to yourself as you go about deciding when and where to propose, or be prepared for one mopey girlfriend.

I'll go into details a little later on why holidays, like Christmas and Valentine's Day, are cliché and not the best days to pop the question but to give you a snippet, besides ruining that day forever should things not work out in the future, you can be certain to blend in with all the other couples who tend to get engaged around the same time.

It's not just holiday's you should be wary of. There are a host of other instances that you should steer clear of when it comes to when and where you elect to propose. Unless you want your good news being overshadowed be mindful of the following events and occasions to avoid piggy backing your proposal off.

Birthdays

Not unlike proposing on a holiday, popping the question on either of your birthdays could be a very bad idea. Besides it just being plain weird that you chose the day you were born to propose—unless you share the same birthday (see: There's no I in Yes), do you like the thought of crying yourself to sleep every year you get older? If she says no, or if you don't live happily ever after, you should prepare for that.

New Babies

Is there a chance of a close friend or sibling giving birth? Push your proposal until after the new baby has arrived and everyone has settled down from that excitement. New babies are big attention grabbers; think baby showers, hospital visits, and then the obligatory at home visit. She won't want to compete with people fawning over her friend's baby pictures instead of her brand new ring.

Other Engagements

You were thinking about proposing on August 8th, but your girlfriend's best friend just got proposed to on August 6th. What to do? I'll tell you what you should definitely NOT do—propose. Make sure other close friends are not getting engaged at the same time if you can.

Unfortunately, there's nothing you can do if a friend decides to propose shortly after you do on a whim or without clueing you in first. Unfortunately, not every guy has read this book.

Sad Event
Death, illness, job loss, natural disaster, foreclosure—all examples of exactly when you should NOT be thinking about popping the question to your loved one. Trying to ease someone's mourning along in this manner is insensitive and inappropriate.

It's natural to want a distraction that will take your focus off bad things that may be happening all around you, but it's no reason to propose. You and your girlfriend should be in the right frame of mind, and have the right motivation.

It's simple, don't try to lump her special moment in with anything else. It deserves its own special time in the sun. Plus, why would you want to limit the opportunities in your life to celebrate only once, when you can have two separate happy occasions to celebrate.

16. The Joke's On You

There are many proposal videos that have gone viral on YouTube. One particularly popular video involves a man staging his death by falling five stories off the roof of their apartment building. Yes, this was original, but there is a reason why people do not typically fake their death during a marriage proposal.

In the video, a secret camera records his girlfriend's reaction as she watches her boyfriend ask a friend to throw him the ring, and then loses balance trying to catch it before tumbling off the ledge of the building. Can you imagine what was going through the poor girl's mind as this happened?

As you watch her reaction in slow motion, a wave of shock, horror, and a million other negative emotions passes over her face as she watches one of the people she loves most in the world go falling to his death mid proposal.

The camera follows her as she rushes to the ledge and sees him lying safely on a foam mattress, with the words "will you marry me?" spelled out. So, after giving his girlfriend a near heart attack, and making her experience one of the lowest feelings humanly possible, he then pivoted the situation and asked for her hand in marriage. Sounds utterly romantic, right? Not so much. Try awkward, painful, and ridiculous.

This is a case of focusing on the surprise element at the detriment of the romantic element. Even if you consider your girlfriend one of the coolest human beings around with the best sense of humor, you can't just ignore that every woman wants her proposal to be romantic and sweet. This popular proposal video is a horrendous mistake for a couple of reasons which I will go through now.

First, with any gag proposal, you have stolen the spotlight. The proposal is no longer about her, it will be laser focused on you, which is a really selfish thing to do and will be a bad precedent to set for your future together. Secondly, you are ignoring the other important factors for a romantic proposal. Remember most women do want to choose between being surprised or being romanced, they want both, with creativity to boot.

Being original, creative, and coming up with an unique proposal is a difficult challenge, especially with the advance of social media and the internet. Even if you do come up with something yourself the chances are that someone else has thought of it first. Don't try to one up the viral proposal videos. It's far better just to draw inspiration and try to come up with something that will impress your lady.

17. From Left Field

This next cardinal proposal mistake some guys foolishly make is popping the question without ever mentioning marriage or testing the waters beforehand. Quite frankly, it's a ballsy and really stupid move. If you respect yourself and have an iota of pride you should gently build up to this moment.

For an idea of how incredibly wrong this could turn out, go to YouTube and search for marriage proposals gone wrong or marriage proposal disasters. If you want to increase your chances of being rejected, embarrassed, wasting money, and killing your relationship, go ahead and spring a proposal without ever broaching the topic with your girlfriend.

"But, I know she wants to get married!" I can hear some of you protesting. How do you know? "I just do!" Not good enough. I really hate to be the bearer of bad news, but just because a woman has been dating you for a length of time doesn't automatically mean she wants to marry you. Similarly, just because she's dating you doesn't mean she believes in marriage at all. Plenty of modern day women are put off by the institution of marriage and have declared that they never want to get married.

The only way you'll know if your girlfriend falls within the scope of women who believe in marriage and is considering marrying you is by having a talk with her. Ideally sometime during the early course of your relationship you should have a talk where you discuss where she stands on marriage, because it's a huge deal and major incompatibility issue if her feelings on marriage don't align with yours.

If she expressed early on that she has no desire to get married, don't just assume she may have changed her mind because you're such an awesome guy.

Similarly, if she said early on that she is looking forward to getting married, don't just assume that she has come to the conclusion that you are the person she wants to take that huge step with. People and their plans have a tendency to change.

I like the saying, when you assume you make an ass out of "you" and "me". Save yourself potential heartache and sure up whether you are likely to get a yes or no by simply having a discussion first.

Section IV- Organization

18. Public or Private

Ok, now that we've gotten through how to make sure you don't ruin the surprise and covering her basic expectations, let's get into the meat and potatoes of the actual marriage proposal.

So many guys get whether to propose privately or publicly wrong, it's pathetic. Considering this is what she is going to remember above all, you honestly cannot afford to screw this up.

Every girl is unique, with different desires and needs. It is your job to know or figure out what type of girl you are asking to marry you. Some girls like to be the center of attention and want nothing more than to be proposed to in front of a big crowd in a public space. Other girls are shy and prefer a more low key, yet still thoughtful, proposal that doesn't put too much of the spotlight on them.

How To Propose Without Screwing It Up

Knowing your girlfriend's personality type and preference will help you avoid embarrassing her in thousands of eyes watching or underwhelming her with a more private intimate proposal inside a hotel room. At the risk of beating a dead horse, you will notice I said your girlfriend's preference and not your own. I can't tell you how many guys have claimed their girlfriends are really private and low key and would not enjoy the spectacle of being proposed to in a big way, when in reality they are the ones not so into the idea of a putting in the effort or making such a grandiose declaration of their feelings in front of a crowd.

Even for those women who insist they don't need anything big, you would be surprised when you start to ask details about what they consider that to actually mean. One woman I spoke to said she didn't need anything elaborate and that she would want her man to keep her marriage proposal simple. When further pressed for details about her dream scenario, she revealed it would be a horse and carriage ride through Central Park, replete with flowers, chocolate, champagne, a picnic thrown, and maybe a surprise violinist in for good measure. Now, you tell me, does that sound anything like a 'simple' request?

As it turned out, her idea of simple was that it didn't need to necessarily be "public" in terms of being in front of a crowd of people, and I found this recurring theme crop up over and over again. Every woman wanted their proposal to reflect thought, creativity and an element of surprise, but some wanted it to be in such a manner that very few people were around, and others wanted the entire world to bear witness to her celebrity moment. In other words, if your woman wants a more private and intimate affair, it doesn't mean you get to surprise her in bed with a mimosa and breakfast and expect her to swoon.

That's all well and good, but what if you have no idea which category the woman you love fits into? If you're not sure, there are clues that will give you a good indication of which path to pursue.

For starters, is she an introvert or extrovert? Extroverts are outgoing, overtly expressive, and social people. They like to put themselves out there and have all eyes fixated on them. If she enjoys dressing up to the nines, going out to the happening places or bigger cities where every one's end goal is to see and be seen, and has a lot of friends, she's probably an extrovert and would prefer a public spectacle. If she is a performer (actor, singer, model) or has chosen a field/job where she is required to be on, and demand a lot of attention, she is most likely going to find your humble, private proposal unsatisfactory.

Introverts, on the other hand, are shy or usually energized by spending time alone. They're more concerned with the inner world of the mind. They enjoy thinking, exploring their thoughts and feelings, and often avoid social situations because being around people drains their energy. It doesn't mean introverts are lacking good social skills. It's just that after being with people for any length of time such as at a party, they need time alone to "recharge".

If the above description fits your girlfriend, it's probably best for you to avoid putting her on the spot in a very public way, because she will not enjoy it as an extrovert would. So exnay on the flash mob proposal.

There is a chance that your girlfriend might exhibit the characteristics of both an extrovert and an introvert, and perhaps you're still not so sure. Don't fret, women are complicated but I have more than a few techniques up my sleeve for sussing out her deepest desires.

Is she the old fashioned type? If your woman enjoys cooking, washing, minding the house, has expressed interested in having a traditional family, and exhibits very feminine characteristics, like taking care of you, she may enjoy a more traditional, intimate marriage proposal. It is only as of late that more and more men have been trying to outdo one another with elaborate proposals involving live television, music videos, celebrities, every friend, family and acquaintance being present, and the like.

One of the easiest ways I would recommend knowing where your girlfriend stands on the barometer of public and private marriage proposals, is to find a way to subtly test her. One day when you're just hanging out with your girlfriend, maybe when you are both in the living room working on your laptops/computers, start playing a video clip of a very public marriage proposal. They can be found readily on YouTube.

Either volunteer to show it to her, or wait until she inevitably asks what you're watching before letting her see the proposal unfold. She might wonder why you're looking at proposal videos, so just mention offhandedly that it was on your Facebook feed a few times so you happened to check it out or so and so sent it to you.

Next, just listen. If she's like most women, she'll probably make some comment about her approval ("Aww, that was so sweet!") or disapproval ("Yikes, I'd never want to be put on the spot like that!") without you having to solicit her opinion. If she does, you're in the money that the way you choose to pop the question won't miss the mark. If she doesn't explicitly say anything, try to read her body language. Smiles or tears equal good, grimaces and flinches equal bad.

The above may not work for you if she knows you never log into Facebook or wouldn't be caught dead watching a marriage proposal video. You'll just have to find another way. One solution is to go out to dinner with a married couple, or find a way to invite or hang out with a married couple. If it's an older couple that's been married forever. like your parents, even better. After dinner, you could mention something about how perfect or 'not perfect', whichever applies, the couple you've just spent the evening dine with are for each other.

Next, say something like, "Did I ever tell you how he proposed? and most likely, she'll say no. Relay the story, amping up the very public aspect of it, or the very low-key aspect of it, and again, try to accurately judge her reactions. Really, talking about this stuff is like cat nip or worm bait for women, so she will probably have a lot to say. If for some reason you've got a really quiet woman you may have to pry.

Use leading questions like, "Romantic, huh?" or "Did you have some fairy tale way you wanted to be proposed to when you were a little girl?" I wouldn't recommend turning it into a serious talk or asking more than one or two leading questions lest she start to become suspicious as to why you're so interested in her opinion all of a sudden.

19. Getting Too Elaborate

Undoubtedly, you've heard of Murphy's Law before in reference to weddings, but this force of nature doesn't only apply towards the big day. In fact, Murphy's Law will probably make an unwelcome appearance on the day of your proposal as well.

In case you're not familiar, Murphy's Law is the second form of thermodynamics, which predicts a tendency to a more disorganized state. More specifically, it is the old adage typically stated as, "Anything that can go wrong, will go wrong".

While there is absolutely nothing wrong with planning a full on elaborate marriage proposal, you should be aware that the more intricate details that need to be organized, overseen or implemented, the higher the chances that something will get overlooked or not pan out according to plan.

There is such a thing as too big, believe it or not! If your plan is excessively creative and ambitious, there is a very real possibility that something will go wrong and it will blow up in your face. You will be left embarrassed and she will be very disappointed that her special day was ruined by some tiny glitch.

By all means you need to be creative but if it is something so unusual there is a good chance it will not work out as planned, reconsider. Remember you get one shot at this (per woman) in your life; there is no second chance to propose to a woman the first time, so it needs to work flawlessly.

20. Relying on The Unreliable

Before you go involving loads of people to pull off your romantic proposal, realize that although this day will be of the utmost importance to you and your fiancé, it probably won't rank as high up there on other people's lists of priorities.

That is not to say that the people you choose to involve won't be happy for you, it just means that you cannot expect others to place the same level of commitment and dedication to making sure everything goes off without a hitch as you will, even if you pay them.

Realize from now that the more other people involved, the more likely things are to go awry. If you need to involve the help of another person (friend, brother, assistant, etc.) you need to make sure that they are very reliable, punctual, prompt. and know how to follow instructions.

Other people's negligence can easily screw up everything. She won't care that it's not your fault; if your assistants and accomplices are incompetent this reflects very badly on you. Be sure to vet your co-conspirators thoroughly, and don't leave anything to chance.

Relying on the unreliable does not only apply to undependable people, but undependable technology, transportation, and weather. Do you really think it's a good idea to trust your friend's car, the one with close to 200,000 miles on it, for the trip to the winery you want to take your girlfriend to?

The same goes for buses and trains, if it's public transportation and you need to be at a location at a specific time, like to catch the airplane that's going to fly your proposal banner over the park at 5pm, give yourself breathing room and arrive early (by the way, 4:50pm is not considered early in this scenario).

21. Proposing on a Holiday

Ah, the inevitable question that will plague your mind once the decision to actually jump in with two feet has struck. Is there a better time of year than others? As it turns out, Christmas is considered one of four big proposal days, along with Valentine's Day, Thanksgiving and New Years. Thirty-nine percent of proposals occurred between November and February among 20,000 newlyweds surveyed by the popular wedding website TheKnot.com. Of those, 16 percent got engaged in December, more than any other month, according to TheKnot editor Anja Winikka.

One can see why, given many of these holidays are considered the most "wonderful" (Christmas), "romantic" (valentine's day), "family oriented" (Thanksgiving) and "celebratory" (New Years) time of the year and all. It would appear another reason for the popularity of tieing a proposal to a specific holiday is knowing you'll to be around family and surrounded by all the people you would want to see and share your exciting news with.

All valid arguments, but I'm sorry to say, when stacking the pros and cons, the cons vastly outweighs any reason to follow the lead of other clueless guys. Just because a lot of men do this, doesn't mean it's right. After all, if all the men jumped off a bridge while proposing, would you do it too? I kid, but as you hopefully realize by now, most guys don't really know what they're doing and their unhappy girlfriends are a testament to this fact.

Trust me, I only want to spare you as much pain as possible. Although I wish you and your wife-to-be a long and happy life together, like ever after if at all possible, I want to protect you from the consequences that could occur should, worst case scenario, you not work out. I hope my advice will never have to apply for you, but it's better to be safe than sorry, right?

Here's the thing with proposing on a holiday like Christmas, Valentine's Days, or even the Fourth of July, for that matter. As sweet as the sentiment is, heaven forbid you and your sweetie decide to part ways three, five, seven or ten years down the line (for some reason these are the years most couples face huge speed bumps in their relationship). Should that happen, the day you proposed and what it represents will be tainted in you and your girlfriend's mind forever.

You and your ex will have a lifetime of misery when that particular holiday rolls along, and it will come like clockwork every single year to break your heart all over again. You won't be able to stop yourself from recalling that fateful day when you proposed, while everyone else around you is in the throes of celebration and happiness. If the proposal had been on any other day, then the probability of remembering the date and getting all torn up about it is slim to none. Zilch, really.

I don't say all of that to say go into your marriage thinking it might fail. I just want you to look beyond the fantasy and acknowledge reality—then prepare accordingly.

Another reason popping the question on a holiday sucks as an engagement day is mostly because so many people get engaged on the same days and an engagement should be a special day in and of itself, not shared with many other "special days" or a holiday. You see, there are guys who propose on a holiday, like Christmas, and the proposal "story" consists of him giving the "gift" of a ring to his fiancé.

Everyone knows that if you're born around a gift-giving holiday, people will try to screw you over with one gift instead of two. Besides being pretty cheap and unimaginative, everyone else she knows will have received a gift. Putting a ring under a Christmas tree does not constitute as "planning" a proposal, it's called giving a Christmas gift in lieu of a separate Christmas gift.

My advice is to elect a date that isn't tied to anything else, and make it your special day. For example, a random weekend in the spring when the weather is projected to be beautiful. Try to avoid proposing on a vacation to your favorite place in the world that you visit every year. Much like proposing on a holiday, if you propose in New York City and your relationship never takes a wrong turn, every time either of you visit or are reminded of the city through advertisements or movies you will remember the proposal by association, awakening those warm fuzzy feelings.

However, if things don't work out, many things can go wrong on a holiday. In this environment you will not be able to plan ahead and scout out the perfect location. Often places are not how you imagined them or what they looked like in the brochure, and often you cannot get access to the specific time you had planned in your head. That said, if you are really diligent and do your homework you may be able to pull it off.

22. Beauty and the Beast

It's the big day, the day you finally drop down on one knee, say it out loud how much she means to you, and ask her to be your wife. You have a huge surprise planned that's going to totally catch her off guard, and she's going to love it because it matches her personality and what she has expressed in the past. Well, wait just one second, because there is a caveat to surprising women that for some reason never crosses men's minds.

Women want to look their best, or at least avoid looking their absolute worst, during the major, special moments in their lives. Just the other day, I happened to be eating in a restaurant in Manhattan, when a reality television crew arrived and started to set up for their shot.

Almost immediately all the women that were in the restaurant started to primp themselves—applying lip gloss and eye makeup, tousling hair, and trying to enhance themselves in the smallest ways possible. You would think every woman in the place was getting ready for her close up, even though they were only going to be in the background. And since they hadn't signed releases, they would probably wind up with their faces being blurred out anyway.

The morale of the story is the majority of women are very image conscious, and if you are going to catch a woman off guard at least give her a decoy to ensure she looks her best. Imagine you've asked your girlfriend to meet you for breakfast and she shows up looking like she has just rolled out of bed, meanwhile you're all primped for the real occasion because you're aware of the videographer on standby, and that an entire crowd of people are about to be staring at you in a matter of moments.

Maybe now you can understand why she may appreciate some forewarning that gives her a reason to look presentable—even if said forewarning is a complete and utter lie.

What about if your proposal is taking place someplace no one will be dressed up? Nope, no dice. Remember, every girl wants to feel like their moment is a big deal. They want to be wowed (not necessarily in public) and celebrate the occasion for a good bit, not have the moment come and go as though nothing significant has occurred.

23. Super Sketchy

We know you don't want to ruin the surprise, and I will tell you upfront that the ring will take up a good chunk of your brain space the days and weeks leading up to your proposal. However, there's a thin line between being romantically secretive and looking guilty as hell.

Women are very attentive to even small changes in your behavior. When you are gearing up for a proposal you will be acting a little different whether you like it or not; mostly anxious, nervous, and unsure. These emotions are strong and sometimes leak out.

Some men, in a crazed effort to make sure she is very surprised, become distant and secretive before the big day. Do not do this, as you will throw her off the scent but not in the way you intended. It will be easy for her to interpret such behavior negatively. She may think you're thinking about leaving her, having an affair, or a host of other worst-case scenario ideas, which could ultimately ruin the proposal.

It will take time to plan it properly and get every little detail sorted and in the right place at the right time. This will mean that you will be spending a good portion of your free time plotting and planning instead of with her. This could easily look like you are spending time with another woman. I know this sounds crazy but that's how woman think.

There are some simple steps to follow in order to not look secretive or suspicious.

Plan months in advance depending on how complex the idea is. If you start early you can do a little at a time and you absence here and there will not be noticed. Additionally, you will be less stressed out since you are giving yourself ample time to plan, and won't sound her alarms.

Work from the office. It's easy to believe that you have to stay late at the office a few nights a week, as long as it's not too late. Also this has the added benefit that she will never stumble upon your receipts, numbers, and proposal related research.

If you need to scout a location bring a friend with you for advice. They can also act as a perfect alibi when she inevitably asks you where you have been all Saturday. If you said you were watching football with the guys and she later asks one of your friends about the game it is too easy for him to slip up if he wasn't with you or evidence of the contrary exists (like his girlfriend posting a picture of them doing something else entirely when he was supposed to be out with you).

24. Getting in Over Your Head

I get it, you want your proposal to be special and give her the memory of a lifetime. I've heard of amazing proposals that have racked up a hefty bill to the tune of thousands of dollars. Now, if money is no object to you and you have deep pockets, by all means, go all out with your proposal. However, if money is tight and you find yourself scrimping on the wedding ring to make a grand proposal, you might want to set your sights on a more economical idea.

You will be hard pressed to find a woman who would welcome you get yourself into financial straits in order to propose in a grand way. There is no need to keep up with the Jones' or compete with anyone else.

Proposing is not a contest of how much money you can burn—save that for the wedding where there will be more witnesses and photographic evidence.

25. Majoring In The Minor

Finally, a common mistake many men make when proposing is to forget the little finer details that can very quickly add up to produce an unforgettable experience. They wrongly figure that the mere fact that they are asking is enough. Yes, it is an amazing gesture to choose someone to commit yourself to for the rest of your life, and flubbing a detail or too won't be a deal breaker for most women, but do this too much and it will result in an overall lackluster experience for your loved one.

I've gone over a lot of what are seemingly minor details throughout the book, so at this point what other details could you possibly have to worry about after all of the above? Think about it this way, you're running a race to the finish line, and you've been leading the pack since the very start. You've come so far already, and the finish line is in sight, but your opponent is starting to pick up speed and could potentially override all your hard work.

Then you recall a tidbit of information from your coach that could make all the different. No, it's not to pick up speed—you're already giving it all you've got.

You implement the trick and it's a photo finish with you the victor. That last trick you had up your sleeve was to outstretch your head, almost diving head first, across the finish line. Yep, you won the race literally by a nose!

Paying attention to the details is like having a secret ace card up your sleeve, guaranteed to put your proposal over the edge. When your girlfriend looks back and reflects on her proposal, she'll realize that you thought of everything, and love you all the more for it. Look, I meant it when I said I set out with a goal to write the definitive book on how to deliver the perfect marriage proposal.

Everything we've covered so far will put a smile so wide on your girlfriend's face, you'll be glad you learned that you needed to think about capturing the moment with a videographer or photographer, or that you should never let anyone else try on your sweetheart's ring. After all, make your sweetheart happy and she'll be inclined to make you happy in return.

The final suggestions below won't cost you much more or in some cases, anything at all, but can make all the difference in her perception of just how excited and dedicated you are to making her happy in the long run. As you read, see how you can implement as much as you can into your proposal.

Music to Her Ears
Most couples have a special song(s) that is meaningful to them. It could be the song that was playing when they locked eyes across the room or locked lips for the first time at a concert, a song that describes your relationship perfectly, or a song by an artist that you both share an unhealthy obsession for.

Making sure to include this song while proposing can take the proposal from an 8 to a 10 in her eyes. Sure, it would be great if you could hire the artist for a live rendition, or just her favorite artist in general, but that can be pretty pricey. A live musician, guitar soloists and violinists are especially popular or a simple mp3 player and speakers will suffice just fine.

Do the Honors
I spoke about getting down on one knee and making sure you have the ring, but don't forget to first, present the ring box, and after she says yes, to put the ring on her finger. The amount of complaints from women about boyfriends who stood around awkwardly while she waited for his lead, or who had to ask if he was "going to put the ring on or what?" is down right sad. Even worse are those women who are forced to take it upon themselves to finish the man's job.

This is one time where you should be in complete control of the situation. It's the ultimate masculine act to propose to a woman, and although she will have standards, she may feel uncomfortable trying to guide you along, so she may keep quiet then. But she'll just turn around and voice her frustrations with you later on or complain to her friends and Internet strangers later.

Use Your Words
It may seem like common sense, but if you want someone to spend the rest of their life with you, you should not assume they will say yes to your question. You have to ask. Simply saying something like, "I can't imagine spending my life without you" is sweet, but doesn't exactly lend itself to a yes or no response; it should always be followed by something they can answer back.

Don't forget that the point of going through all you have to create a special moment is for you to ask a very important question. I have encountered countless stories of men who displayed the ring and then forgot to actually say those four magical words, "Will you marry me?" or some other version, such as, "Will you make me the happiest man alive and marry me?"

These are the words that your girlfriend has been waiting with bated breath to hear. Either way you choose to phrase it, just be sure you actually give her a reason to scream or sob "Yes!", which is what officially makes you an engaged couple: the offer and the acceptance.

To wrap up the moment perfectly, be sure to express your delight by hugging and kissing her or saying, "I love you" after everything has been said and done. You can't get anymore romantic by sealing such a profound moment with a good kiss.

Section V - The Ring Thing

26. Dude, Where's My Ring?

In a survey conducted by TheKnot.com and Men's Health, which involved a total of 3,000 men and women, 1/3 of brides-to-be expressed not being fans of men who propose without a ring. Shocking, right? Unless your girlfriend has flat out said, "I don't want an engagement ring" she wants an engagement ring. Proposing without a ring to a woman who is expecting one is like stepping up to the baseball plate without a bat. You definitely won't be hitting any home runs in either situation.

Granted, there are some women who express the desire to have a say in choosing the ring, but this doesn't give you an excuse to show up empty handed. Placeholder or stand-in rings do the job nicely of putting something on her finger to symbolize the magnitude of the deed being done.

A heart-shaped mood ring, something you personally make (if you're good at stuff like that), a ring passed on in your family, a gemstone ring with super sparkly "stones" in her favorite color, or a ring that has some sort of symbolic relevance are all excellent alternatives to the empty handed approach. Almost anything will be cute and she'll enjoy wearing it until she gets the real one she has already communicated she wants to design or choose.

For the other ⅔ of women who thought it unpolitically correct or unfeminist to admit to wanting a man to pop the question with an added motivator to say yes, a bit more time and effort is required. You have to understand, there's something innately incomplete about a marriage proposal without a ring. Ever since Archduke Maximillian of Austria gave a diamond ring to Mary of Burgundy in 1477, the tradition of diamond engagement rings took on a life of its own.

Of course, the commercial jewelers have poured a lot of time and money into advertising messages that perpetuate the idea that a ringless proposal is a subpar one. It's not right, but the reality is that's what you are up against, and again this is not the best time to stick it to the man or make a statement about consumerism in America.

Pinpointing who's to blame for what society considers standard etiquette won't change much. The woman you want to be your wife will probably be of the same mindset of the majority of ladies who have come to envision a certain image when being proposed to; that of a man offering a box with a sparkly diamond. The fact that she will automatically get bombarded with questions and requests to fawn over the ring from friends and family once they find out she is engaged adds to the pressure for you to step up to the plate correctly if you're going to step up at all.

27. Size Matters

It bears clarifying, the above should not be used as an excuse to prolong your proposal or skimp on a ring. The old saying of saving up two month's worth of salary is not a hard and fast rule that you need to comply with. If you can't afford a blinged out ring, getting something that you can afford is definitely better than nothing.

However, don't think for a second that a reasonable woman won't be expecting a reasonably sized diamond. If you get the ring right, it won't matter that it's slightly smaller than the huge rock promoted as the ultimate engagement ring. Chances are it will suffice in the eyes of the woman who loves you. However, that doesn't give you a license to pick up a diamond that could pass as your five-year-old niece's first stud earrings. Let's be real here—size does matter.

It all boils down to your budget and being savvy with your dollar bills. www.mint.com is a easy and free way to budget for a ring. You can enter the amount you want to save and the target date of purchase, and mint will create a personalized budget plan for you and indicate exactly what you need to sacrifice in order to reach your goal. Plan ahead and save up, and work within your budget to purchase the best ring that you can afford.

For those of you who don't mind doing a bit of extra legwork to get a ring that will be sure to impress her and her friends, there are countless resources that exist that will enable you to score a pretty gem without heading straight for the poor house afterwards.

Yes, a smaller ring presented in the famous baby blue Tiffany's box will leave a girl googley-eyed, but a sizeable rock will quickly overshadow the fact that the box doesn't boast some huge brand name. The takeaway is that if you are working with limited funds and want to impress her and everyone else who lays eyes on her rock, stay far away from the name brand jewelry stores and big box retailers. That is, unless you don't mind the cost of their rent, hefty advertising budget, and staff built in to the cost of your ring.

If you want even more bang for your buck, here are some additional tips your jeweler won't tell you: When buying a diamond, you are told to keep in mind the four c's - clarity, cut, color and carat weight. Consider clarity—having a flawless ring isn't necessary. Inclusions determine price, but many flaws are visible only under 10X magnification.

Turning to the Internet is a savvy ring shopper's best option. The list of resources available are just about endless. Be smart though as not all Internet websites are created equally. Craigslist, Amazon and E-bay wouldn't be my first recommendation. With Craigslist, scam artists abound and there is absolutely no protection. If you get screwed over with a purchase, Mr. Craig won't be there to make things right, and you'll be up a creek without a paddle with useless costume jewelry.

Despite the huge presence of Amazon and E0bay, you won't fare much better with their protection policies either. For example, Amazon will tell you to contact the vendor if you have an issue with the ring, and the insurance 'protection' from E-bay/Paypal will only cover your purchase up to a certain amount. Plus, if a transaction goes wrong the hassle of not getting what you anticipated when you anticipated it could force you to push back and delay your plans, which can be an extra expense if you've booked dates and paid deposits.

A safer bet is to turn to individual websites that focus on selling jewelry or engagement jewelry. You will have more options to select from, additional proof in the form of certification reports from a major lab such as the GIA or AGS that your item is what it purports to be, and much more reasonable prices since there won't be as much overhead and fixed costs with running the site as compared to brick and mortar stores. When you remove the middlemen, you benefit.

Finally, and I recognize some of you won't be all that comfortable with this one, but there are websites that re-sell engagement rings for couples who have called off their weddings or walked down the path of divorce. The stigma is that buying such a ring will curse your relationship to the same fate as the previous owners, but that is pure nonsense. Every day divorced men and women resell their jewelry from their failed engagement or marriage at a loss to jewelers who shine the ring back up and put it on their sales floor for a much higher price, with buyers none the wiser.

The difference is you know the backstory for sites that advertise their niche upfront in order to gain more exposure and attract the appropriate audience. You also pay less because these individual owners are motivated to get rid of something that reminds them of their failed romance, and get whatever monetary compensation they can in the process.

If you go this route, I absolutely wouldn't recommend divulging the source of your purchase to your fiancé. Chances are, she won't ask anyway.

For those of you looking for a bit more detail in the form of website recommendations and links, I've intentionally omitted them since the internet is not static, with new big players popping up daily and older websites closing at the same rate. Instead of putting in a bunch of links that may not be active when you come across this book, I recommend using Google as your friend.

28. Getting It All Wrong

So you got a ring to illustrate your seriousness and commitment to marrying the woman you love. That's great! Unfortunately, there's one other thing you have to consider if you don't want to be met with a disapproving flash across her face, before she tries to conceal her true feelings. Does the ring fit her, literally and figuratively, or does she absolutely hate it and dreads the thought of having to wear it for the rest of her life?

Yes, you should not show up unprepared to ask with a ring in tow, but any old ring is not going to cut it. If a girl is not fond of the ring you choose for her, she is reminded every time she looks down at her fingers of a bad feeling—a feeling of things not being right; a feeling of wishing she could take off the ring or wondering if you're the right guy.

It may seem nonsensical, but in their minds, the right guy would pick out the right ring. It's kind of like how women think it's a sign when it rains on their wedding day—a ring that falls off her finger or is hideous in her opinion, gets assigned a much deeper meaning than you might give it.

That's why the number five mistake most men make while proposing is to get the ring all wrong. Don't be that guy.

Since you don't want her associating such negative thoughts with you, the best way to get the ring right is to find out beforehand what your woman's ring preference is. Obviously, you won't want to try to slip in such a question the day you go to purchase the ring. Ideally, you would have asked her months in advance. However, if it's drawing close to crunch time, another way to figure out her preference is to do some digging.

Quietly observe the type of jewelry she usually wears to get a hint of her likes. If she doesn't wear much jewelry, take notice of the one or two pieces she does have. At least you'll know for sure she is fond of that style. If she wears a lot of jewelry, try to pinpoint the one she wears the most, her favorite piece. With women who have a lot more jewelry, you have a smaller chance of screwing it up since you have a more varied range of styles to choose from—that is if all of the rings are not similar in style.

Another stealth way of gathering information is to compliment her on the piece when she is wearing it and ask her if it's her favorite since she wears it so often, or ask her why she wears that particular piece so much. Inquire what she likes about it and take a mental note. Most women will like the cut, style or color of the gem. Although, keep in mind that opting for chocolate or yellow diamonds because she likes that color on her ordinary rings is a risky move. A white diamond is the standard amongst engagement rings.

If you think you'll have a hard time describing the ring to the jeweler, get a quick snapshot of the piece on your phone when she isn't looking. Simply do the making a fake phone call or looking up something in your phone maneuver, make sure your sound is turned off so she won't hear the clicking of a photo being taken, and zoom in on her finger. If you have untethered access to her jewelry box, go ahead and take as many pictures of her rings as you can for inspiration.

In fact, we recommend finding a way to seize the ring for a day trip to the local jeweler. Try not to take a ring she will miss, like her absolute favorite ring that she might be inclined to put on at a moments notice. Similarly, don't take it before she has gotten dressed and left the house. If she's already gone for the day and left the ring behind it's a much safer bet.

Be sure to replace the ring as soon as you can to lessen the chances of her noticing its M.I.A status. You wouldn't think with the amount of jewelry some women possess they'd notice when one ring has gone missing, but you'd be surprised.

Your trip to the jewelers will serve as a means of figuring out her ring size, so that you can be sure the ring will actually fit her when you place your order online or in the store. Remember, if you're budget conscious and want to get the best bang for your buck, you'd do well to avoid buying the ring at high-end jewelry stores. Even a mom and pop jewelry store will be more open to working with you and giving you a decent price.

While you're at the jewelry store, feel free to utilize the salesperson for guidance on the right style and cut that she will be sure to appreciate. They'll tell you the official names of cuts and what's in trend, which will make your on or offline comparison shopping endeavor a lot easier since you'll be able to drill down to the exact specifications you are looking for. Take all of the information they give you into consideration when deciding on your final purchase, and if you feel bad about not buying the diamond from them while mining them for information, you can always give them your business for your wedding bands or some other present for your lady (or mother), which will generally be a lot cheaper.

Another way to discover your honey's jewelry taste without outright asking and ruining the surprise is to enlist the help of the Internet. First, start off with Amazon's handy little feature called 'wishlist'. Everyone who has an account on amazon has the ability to compile what is called a wish list, or an online aggregator of items they've come across that they'd like to buy, but for one reason or another cannot buy immediately.

Finding an amazon wish list is as simple as going to http://www.amazon.com/gp/wishlist or Googling 'amazon wish list'. On the home page you will find a section that allows you to search for a wish list by a person's name or email address. Since searching by name could yield a lot of results if your girlfriend has a common moniker, it is best to start your search off by entering her e-mail address. Scan her list for jewelry and rings to get a clear-cut idea of the type of rings she would enjoy.

If your girlfriend hasn't discovered the Amazon wish list tool, your next best bet is to check out pinterest.com Pinterest is a haven for superior seekers and curators of the finer things in life to congregate. A whopping 87% of US sign ups to Pinterest has been from women, according to data from comScore. Female users dominate the site and chances that your one and only has discovered the site are high.

This works out perfectly in your favor as it provides another resource for you to potentially gather information on her ring preferences without outright asking. Much like Amazon's Wish list, you can search by first and last name, but the more accurate and simple way to find a specific individual on pinterest is to search for their e-mail or use Facebook.

Go to pinterest.com and enter her email address into the search bar at the top of the page. If the search yields no results, near the top of the page you will be able to see pins, board, and people. Click people and you'll be able to locate her account should she have one.

If that doesn't work because she has updated her privacy settings so that she cannot be found publicly or has signed up with an email address you're not familiar with, you can still try Facebook. As long as you are Facebook friends, after signing up for a Pinterest account, go to find friends in the drop down menu under your username and log into Facebook. You will be able to see if she has an account.

One other option, which I'd recommend as the last resort, is to ask for advice from a friend or family member that knows her well. Truthfully speaking, her friends and family probably won't be able to offer much more insight than if you were to spend the time to observe what she has already said she likes with her purchasing dollars. It truly is the lazy man's way out and won't guarantee she'll be happy. It also just opens you up to the possibility of her being leaked your secret, but in some circumstances, like if you are long distance and don't have access to her jewelry collection, a friend or family member can come in handy.

In the end, she'll be pleasantly surprised that you know her taste, or cared enough about appealing to her taste to go through the trouble of sleuthing around. Trust me when I say, getting the ring right will make all the difference between her saying yes and meaning it, and is worth the extra effort.

29. Ring Flubs

Ah, the engagement ring. A symbol of love and a promise to stay true to your future spouse. Something shiny to show off to your friends. Much has already been covered about it, like the fact that you absolutely should not even think about proposing without the best ring your budget can afford, or at least a placeholder if she has expressed wanting to design or pick out her own.

If you think buying and remembering to bring the ring is the only potential for screwing up your proposal, I've got news for you. From where to hide the ring, to how to deliver it, there is a lot of confusion and ambiguity that leads plenty of room for screw-ups.

Hiding the Ring in Food
Darn! Were you hoping this wouldn't be on the list? Who hasn't heard of the marriage proposal that involves slipping the ring in a glass of champagne, or a baked good and waiting for your girlfriend to discover it? The idea is, she will have no choice but to notice the huge sparkly diamond at the bottom of her flute, or buried in her dessert. She'll go crazy once she realizes that you're proposing and be bowled over by your enormous gesture. As I'm sure you can tell, I'm being totally facetious.

First, despite what you may have been told, this is not romantic in a woman's eyes. Where's the thought and creativity in dropping a ring in champagne or food? How can it be remotely construed as being personalized to fit her or your relationship? Easy, it doesn't. Second, it's been done a million times before in movies and TV shows. Chances are high that your girlfriend would dread having to share this proposal story with friends and family, and if she doesn't want to share it you can rest assured you've received an F for lack of effort.

How about the logistics? Did you ever stop to think how she would get the ring out? Will you or your girlfriend plop your fingers in your expensive glass of champagne to fish out the ring? Are you going to lick the cake icing off the ring before putting the sticky mess on her finger? Note cute at all.

Next is the issue of hygiene. If you haven't sterilized the ring between touching it to put in the champagne glass, which is darn near impossible to do, her beverage or dessert will not be the model of cleanliness. If your girlfriend is super squeamish about these things, she'll hate it all the more.

Finally, the biggest reason against involving mixing the ring and food in your proposal is the potential injury factor. The hazard risk is pretty high up there that she will not notice the ring and swallow it or chew on the gem, resulting in a trip to the emergency room or dentist when you ought to be celebrating.

Involving Babies and Animals
Another fairly common way to proposal, which a lot of guys think would be a great idea, is to attach the ring on a cat, dog or any other animal's collar. Perhaps the thought is to earn bonus points from the cuteness of the animal and make you look kind and caring.

If you think this is a cute way of popping the question, it's probably best if you went back to the drawing board. First and foremost, this shouldn't even be a consideration if your girlfriend hasn't expressed or displayed that she is a huge fan of animals. If she is afraid of many animals, couldn't care less about them, think they smell gross or wrinkles her nose at the thought of getting animal fur all over her outfit, abort.

Next, how subdued or well behaved is the animal? Is it professionally trained or could it start acting all crazy at any given moment? If you aren't sure or the answer is "no," so should your answer be to whether or not you should use them. You want this moment to be foolproof and as much in your realm of control as possible.

On the other hand, if she has been dying to adopt a puppy or rode and loved horses all her life, then maybe you could consider implementing them in your proposal in some way, like taking her horseback riding, while keeping the ring in your possession at all times. The point is you don't want to rely on the animal for such a special moment. Besides, you want her fawning all over you, not her brand new pup.

Not Hiding the Ring
Every girl knows if her man buys a diamond or equally expensive ring, he is planning on proposing sometime in the very near future. Keep the element of surprise on your side, by making sure to keep the ring out of your girlfriend's sight by any means possible.

This is harder to do if you live together, but not impossible. Find somewhere safe outside of the house that you can stash the ring. This doesn't mean you should go burying it in the yard or someplace someone else is likely to find it. When I say keep it out of the house, I mean with someone you can trust, like your parents' place.

Other terrible hiding places include your car, under the mattress, in a drawer, coat pocket, or anywhere else she frequents. One of the safest places to keep the ring is in the store. Also, do not make the mistake of hiding the ring and forgetting where you've put it or changing its location so many times that you lose track of where you last placed it. Come up with a really good hiding spot and put the ring there as close to the actual proposal date as possible.

Proposing in any way that is likely to wind up with a missing ring is pretty bad since it's a multi-thousand dollar investment that you probably can't afford to lose all willy nilly. Whether you are hiding the ring or presenting it to her, ask yourself what could go wrong and think hard and long about the answers.

Skimping on the Ring
As mentioned before, if you can't afford the hope diamond your girlfriend is probably not going to hold it against you. However, if you can afford a nice ring and skimp on the purchase, she is going to notice and question your motives. Again, it's not that you're obligated to empty your bank account for a piece of jewelry, but if you're emptying it for other purchases, like electronic gadgets, trips with the buddies, etc. and then present an unimpressive ring, don't think she'll be impressed.

Similarly, if you make a good amount of money and buy yourself very nice things, but try to spend as little as possible on her ring, you'll be very successful in making her think you don't want to invest in her because you're hedging your bets (if things don't work out you're not out a bunch of money on her ring).

She will also be quite embarrassed to show off the ring to her friends and family, who more than likely will all be aware of your lifestyle, income, and previous high roller spending habits. Thus, they won't be convinced of your seriousness either, and if they're smart, advise her accordingly.

30. For Her Finger Only

One of the cardinal rules of buying a ring for your future wife is to never let another person try it on before she does. Be careful because some women you show it to will have a desire to put it on their finger to see how it feels to wear something so beautiful.

You will hear phrases like:
"It won't do any harm," or "She will never find out.."

If you do not ignore these warnings you will be playing with fire. For example look at it this way, you arrive home from work and your girlfriend has surprised you with a Ferrari. Wow that would be amazing, you would feel very impressed and would love to return the gesture. Next, her brother comes to visit and tells you he took it for a spin before she gave it to you. Boom! Immediately, the gloss is suddenly wiped clean off the experience.

The same rules apply to a ring. The reason why it's not okay is because if you are giving it to her, it is hers and hers. It's not your place to decide who gets to give her ring a test drive. She will later gladly show off her ring and they wouldn't dare ask her to try it on.

Another less obvious occurrence, and somewhat rare one, is if one of your friends or you are tempted to try the ring on, it might not be as easy to take off. Rings are made for little feminine fingers. Engagement rings are also expensive, delicate, and can be damaged easily.

Another humongous mistake, even worse than allowing any of your friends to try on her ring, is to recycle a ring that you gave to an ex-girlfriend with your current one. Usually second hand rings mean bigger gems, better settings, and fabulous prices, but giving a ring you picked out, based on your ex's tastes and preferences, to a completely different woman is not only creepy and tacky, but stingy.

She'll wonder if you simply chose her because she had the right ring size. Furthermore, your actions will not be a good sign of things to come - will she always get sloppy seconds? It screams that you couldn't be bothered, even if that wasn't your intention.

For example, perhaps you consider the ring as a token of your intention to marry more than anything, or maybe you couldn't afford a new ring after shelling out thousands of dollars on the old one.

I see where you're coming from, but in the former situation, most women simply won't agree with you, and in the later situation where you were lucky enough to get the ring back from your ex, pawn it or sell it online or back to the jewelers. Then use the sales to fund your new girlfriend's ring.

There's no need to hold on to a ring from an ex who denied your proposal for marriage, unless you are doing so because your ex has passed. Still, most women just won't be comfortable with the idea of wearing a ring meant for another woman you presented it to. The only exception where she won't mind wearing another woman's ring is if it's a family heirloom.

Why would she want to wear a reminder of your past love for another woman and constantly wonder if you would be with her if your ex hadn't said no (or why the ex said no in the first place)? So, even if the chances of her finding out are slim, do right by your girlfriend and give her the same respect you'd want her to give to you.

Section VI - Nailing The Proposal

31. Go Big or Go Home

Before you think that I'm saying you have to break the piggy bank and think of a marriage proposal so good it gets over a million hits on YouTube, let me quickly mention that no one expects you to deliver "the best proposal ever", as decided by the world. It is not necessary to put that kind of pressure on your shoulders. The only person you really need to impress is your girlfriend, not the potential viewers on the Internet.

Go big or go home also doesn't mean that your proposal needs to be a very public affair involving set pieces, camera crews, or celebrity appearances. What it does mean, is that the way you propose should be something big in her eyes, because asking someone to marry you should kind of be a big deal.

I touched on it a little before, but I'll iterate now that when your girlfriend insists that she wants you to keep it simple, it doesn't mean she is asking you to not put any effort into it the proposal all. Nor is it an excuse to casually give her a ring in an unremarkable way.

In most instances, those words mean she doesn't want you to think you need to spend your entire life savings on the way you propose to her, or orchestrate a very complex or public affair. Women who are conscious and care about your finances are being sweet and considerate, but they, just like every other girl, doesn't want to be robbed of this exciting, once in a lifetime (hopefully) experience.

The advice to "go big" means you should go big on creativity and forget about the predictable, cliché ways of proposing that have been done to death. Planning something "romantic" that she has probably seen or heard of a thousand times before on a movie screen or read about in cheesy romance novels, will only highlight how little forethought you have put into making the proposal extra special for her. You might think you'll be her knight in shining armor by going the 'classic' route, but you'd be sadly mistaken.

No woman wants to feel like you copied and pasted a proposal because you couldn't be bothered spending a bit of brainpower on what would really appeal specifically to her. You know your sweetheart best, and should have a good grasp of what will impress her and what will let her down, as you begin to carve out your "go big" moment.

The great news is you can draw inspiration from classical marriage proposals and spruce them up to make them 'go big' rather easily. Let the formulaic idea be your base and build on it from there. Here are some examples of "go home" proposals, and how you can make them better by thinking a little bigger.

Proposing Over Dinner
You tell your sweetheart that you're going out for dinner one night. During the course of your meal, or during dessert, you slide the box across the table, maybe get down on one knee, and ask her to marry you. Some patrons of the restaurant cheer and you might think you've nailed it, but there's a very good chance she's going to put on a facade of being impressed to not hurt your feelings when she is feels secretly underwhelmed.

Even writing the above description made me yawn and start to nod off. This is an overdone, typical, and boring story for her to share with her friends. Remember, you'll both be telling people for the rest of your lives how your proposal went down, and "He proposed over dinner" is hardly going to leave an impression that you went all out on anyone—especially your girlfriend.

You can make the cliché act of proposing over dinner "big", by spending a few extra minutes thinking and an additional couple of hours planning and making phone calls. For example, if your girlfriend loves a specific type of food, be sure that the restaurant is one of the best sources in town for this food. If it's a hard restaurant to get in, that's even better. Why? Because it shows beyond the shadow of a doubt that you had to exert effort and book months in advance to get a reservation.

Don't just stop there, though. If she loves a specific dish, arrange with the restaurant in advance to cook a special meal full of her favorite things. You could get even more creative and request the restaurant draw up a special menu that only you and she will receive with those items on it. If the restaurant does not oblige, ask if it would be okay for you to have a special menu printed, that you would pay for, and that they would hand only to the two of you.

If the restaurant has a live band or musical act, you could also arrange beforehand for them to play your special song, or provide them with a list of songs that have had some significant meaning throughout the course of your relationship. Request the act come to your table to serenade your girlfriend or clear it with the restaurant to bring in your own musician (guitar player or violinist) to strum a lovely tune.

Alternatively, you could ask about renting out the restaurant or a back room for the evening. Or arrange for a spotlight on the two of you when it comes time to propose. Or have her family and friends inconspicuously seated behind her and cheering when she says yes. Do you see where I'm going here?

Here's another example of how you can take a blaze proposal and kick it up a notch.

Proposing on the Beach
Let's use the classic (ahem: boring and overdone) idea of taking your girlfriend on a walk on the beach to propose. Hopefully, it's a warm and sunny day, the beach is somewhat secluded, or at least not overcrowded; you stop for a second, drop to one knee, recite a few words and present her with the ring.

Sounds lovely, right? Yes, and I'm sure the first girl to ever be proposed to in this manner found such a proposal to be adequate enough. However, this way of asking a woman to marry you is seen as old news and trite in this day and age. Especially since with only a little bit more time and energy, you can provide your girlfriend with a truly memorable experience that will leave no doubt in her mind that proposing wasn't just an afterthought.

Here are some ways in which you could take the 'beach proposal' to a higher level. Plan for a romantic picnic on the beach, where you provide the food and beverages. Afterwards suggest going for a walk towards a very secluded part of the beach. Not before long, you come across a path, maybe a 'yellow brick road' drawn in the sand that seems to go on forever. The path will eventually lead to a beautiful sand castle, which you would have hired a professional sand sculptor (yes, these people exist) to build or built yourself if you have the skills.

The castle would display the words 'will you marry me' engraved in it, and ideally would not be clearly visible to your fiancé until you get close. As you walk down the path, you could use the opportunity to tell her how much she means to you, recite stories of how you felt when you first laid eyes on her, or instances when you realized she was the one for you.

Your footpath could contain a note every few feet (either a drawing or words marked in the sand), e.g. a different thing about her that you love, which you would then expound upon.

Now, which one do you think will be more likely to stir the emotions inside your girlfriend? Pulling off a proposal like this doesn't have to cost you thousands of dollars either, especially if you are good with your hands and can build the sand castle yourself. To ensure a beach that isn't littered with people trying to soak up the sun, you could elect to go on a weekday or night, just use votive candles to light the path.

Recall what I mentioned about the trend of more and more men spending thousands of dollars on their proposals. Men are doing so because they think women equate the amount of money spent on the proposal with the amount of love he has for her, not unlike how many women equate the amount of money spent on the diamond demonstrates a man's love.

However, what those guys are missing is that it's not just about the money, but the thought and thoughtfulness that impress women about their grand gestures. It just so happens the way those guys have chosen to express the fact that they've put thought and thoughtfulness in the proposal is to spend money.

I like to use the example of a big company with tons of money to spend simply throwing it around to make a 30 second commercial spot at the Super Bowl, versus a small company that doesn't have as big of an advertising budget getting really creative because they have to make every dollar count. Those smaller budget ads surprisingly make ten times the impact of the open-ended budget ads that utilize special effects, celebrities, and the like. Simply, they have no choice but to use more creativity brainpower in order to make their ad impactful so that the exorbitant cost of advertising pays off.

This is not said to discourage you from spending as much money as you want on your marriage proposal. If you can afford it, you can really do some amazing things. You could have fireworks go off for your beach proposal, rent a projector and screen a slide show on the wall of the restaurant, or hire a flash mob to break out in song and dance, if you had a huge budget to work with.

The point of stressing that spending a lot of money is not necessary, is because for the majority of men reading this, you won't have an unlimited source of funds to draw upon. Besides, your girlfriend might not be too pleased to learn she can't have the amazing wedding she has always dreamed of because you blew all of your money on proposing.

I want you to take away this simple fact—the more you do to sweep her off her feet, the more memorable, interesting and personal the proposal story becomes, but sweeping off her feet doesn't require you go into debt.

Nothing stings quite as much as hearing your fiancé or wife dismiss the way you chose to propose, and she won't have a choice but to give a banal description of your actions if it rings true.

Rest assured that she won't give a one line answer of "he proposed on the beach", if you add in the go big elements like the ones suggested above. Instead, she'll excitedly recount how you took the time to arrange a picnic on the beach and then suggested a walk, which led to a yellow brick road sand path, with all the things you love about her in each brick. She'll describe how you then surprised her by having the path stop at a huge sandcastle, which she loved making as a child, that had 'will you marry me' engraved in it.

She'll take pleasure in retelling the story over and over again because she'll be reliving all the wonderful emotions she felt that day every time she does. Every time she recalls how you proposed, she will be reminded of how much she is loved and why she loves you. Give her the opportunity to share why her proposal was different by adding in extra elements that will make the moment bigger. Offer more than just a mere proposition; offer her your heart by putting it into the way you choose to propose.

Otherwise, you stand the risk of her resenting you and feeling like she wasn't special enough to you to warrant more. Even if she says yes, she'll always wonder what it would be like to be one of the lucky girls whose husbands 'got it'; 'it' being the fact that every woman wants to feel extra loved and cherished on this day.

The effort a guy puts into a proposal is a demonstration of the effort he wants and is willing to commit to the relationship, just like your actions (where you spend your time and money) reflect where your priorities lie. Put as much effort and spend whatever money it takes to make the moment say clearly and loudly, "I am willing to invest everything I've got in you. You are worth it to me. You are priceless."

32. Timing Is Everything

Once you've made the decision to propose, and have a ring burning a hole in your pocket, it can be tempting to unload the enormous anxiety bubbling up inside by proposing the first chance you get. Don't worry; you're not alone. Countless men feel the same way, and to their girlfriend's horror, do just that.

Thanks to this book, you'll know better than to make the same mistake. Nothing should compel you to ask before the moment is right or without a carefully thought out plan. You'll both be telling your marriage proposal story for the rest of your lives, and don't want the situation to be memorable for all the wrong reasons, do you? I thought so.

Getting it Over With
Sigh. It is with great sadness to report how eager some men are to stop carrying around their big secret that they neglect to wait for a special moment. I've heard stories of women who were proposed to while in the shower, doing taxes, watching television, cooking dinner, etc.

It's obvious that these men have no respect for timing or the art of proposing marriage, otherwise they would never chose the mundane and completely inappropriate moments they do to pop the question.

It's not charming that you couldn't wait. It spells laziness and that you've only thought about yourself. Your girlfriend deserves better than this.

Proposing After an Argument
I want to tell you a story about a guy named Phil, who had been dating his girlfriend, Ally, for over three years. Ally had made it known that she wanted a proposal soon, so Phil went out and got an engagement ring.

A few weeks later Phil had a modest proposal planned and came home ready to surprise his girlfriend when he was met with a sulky surprise of his own. It turned out a friend of Ally had gotten engaged the day before, and this couple had only been dating for under a year and a half. Understandably, Ally was stewing about her present situation with Phil and the fact that it seemed Phil would never propose.

One thing led to another, and before Phil knew it he and Ally were having a heated argument. Outraged that Ally was raking him over the coals about proposing, which he ironically had planned to do that very day, Phil pulled out his pocket and angrily presented the ring. Needless to say, Ally wasn't impressed.

No, it won't be a funny story to recall after some years have passed. It's a terrible way to enter into such an important chapter of your life. Respect the sanctity of marriage and make the moment you propose be a happy and joyous one, not one filled with anger.

The moral of the story is to not only avoid proposing on a whim because you want to get it over with already, but to consider the timing of when you propose carefully. Every moment has an energy to it: positive or negative. There should be no negative energy surrounding your proposal.

If the circumstances aren't right, abort and go back to the drawing board because once you've proposed, you can't undo or redo the proposal. Plenty relationships have been the victim of proposals gone awry, as both individuals realize that such a shaky start doesn't spell a long and secure future.

Whether you get that urge to spit it out because you're nervous or she's upset that it hasn't happened yet, bite your lip. This is the biggest commitment of your life so think before you do something you regret.

Remember the old saying 'timing is everything'; it could easily equal the difference between a proposal she remembers forever and one she would rather forget. Blurting out, "WILL YOU MARRY ME!" when your girlfriend is dealing with period cramps, has had a terrible day, is pissed at you, or is doing something mundane (like taking a shower) won't be the biggest motivator to get the 'yes' you hopefully seek.

33. The Goldilocks Effect

How soon is too soon to ask a woman to be your wife? If you base the answer on the actions of some men, you'd think it was never or not soon enough, and you'd be very mistaken.

We've all heard about the stories of couples that only date for a few weeks or months before the guy declares his undying love and proposes marriage. Sure, the tales that are passed on from mouth to mouth are those instances where the woman accepts, and that is because it is so rare for an acceptance to be the outcome. What you don't hear about are all the other more common instances where the woman gets freaked out and dumps her boyfriend or starts fading away slowly.

Despite what you may have been led to believe, not every single woman is waiting with bated breath to become engaged, get married and start a family with the first guy that asks. Even if the woman you are dating does want to do all of that one day, it doesn't mean she isn't going to be picky about whom she chooses as her long-term mate.

Everything has a due course or a natural process, and

love and marriage is no different. Your relationship needs to be watered and nurtured so that it can then blossom before it blooms. For a woman, time is essential to sussing out those guys who may say and do all the right things at first, only to reveal their true colors after a few weeks, months, or years have passed.

You should also want time for the same exact reasons. You may think she's got it all: brains, beauty and she's even more into *Breaking Bad* than you. She's 'perfect' and you're understandably eager to take her off the market ad seal the deal after four weeks of dating her, but you may want to do cool your jets until you're beyond the dizzy with infatuation stage.

Everyone tends to be on his or her best behavior at the start of a relationship. You won't be truly ready for a lifetime commitment until you've tackled some real relationship challenges, weathered your beloved's every mood, and received unequivocal signs that she's equally ready to commit. Popping the question too early may result in an awkward "let me think about it and get back to you..." response, or ruin the possibility of ever proposing to her again since you will have scared her off.

Even if she says yes, you have more to lose than she does if either of you change your minds after getting more insight to make an informed decision. After all, you'll be the one shelling out the dough for a ring and a noteworthy proposal. Do you want to be the guy that fails her litmus test after jumping the gun to buy a ring and plan an elaborate proposal for her?

Both of you need to be sure—not just you. She won't be expecting a proposal from you early on, because there's no way for her to be sure about you besides letting the test of time do it's job, so relax a bit, will you? Depending upon a woman's age, she won't start thinking about marriage until at least a year or a year and a half of dating.

Generally speaking, the younger the woman, the less marriage will be on her mind. The older the woman, if she's never been married before, the more marriage will be at the forefront of her thoughts. If an older woman has been married before and done the whole family thing, she might be less inclined to jump back into the fray right away.

I get that the new stages of a relationship can feel wonderful and you want to hold on to the woman responsible for putting you on cloud nine. However, you must realize that you are only in limerence, and you need to go through some stuff together to see how you fare afterwards.

Some milestones you should try to share before going for the kill are: spending Christmas together with each others family, going on at least two vacations, having at least one argument or disagreement, and if your beliefs support it, living together for a few months. If you are able to navigate all of the above with your 'I don't want to live without her' feelings still in tact, then it's safe to proceed.

34. Strike While the Iron is Hot

You will agree that it is very important to be 100% sure that this is the woman you want to spend the rest of your life with before you go through all the bother of planning the perfect proposal. However, you don't have all the time in the world to figure it out. If you wait too long she will get frustrated with your lack of certainty and she might dump you. Don't say I didn't warn you of this mistake when a few months down the line she's got a new man on her arm, and his ring on her finger.

Let's be frank. The majority of women will begin to contemplate marriage a year or so into a relationship. It is at this point she will decide if she wants you to ask her, and if she does determine she wants to marry you, there is a limited amount of time she will be willing to wait for you to suck up the courage and mirror the same level of commitment.

If this seems illogical to you, look at it from her perspective. Yes, all women want a great, fun boyfriend who is interesting to hang out with, however at a certain point in the relationship they begin to look for something else. We'll call this the Father Factor.

There will come a time when she will ask herself, is this man good enough to be the father of my children? As you can imagine the criteria for continuing to be in a relationship changes from simply being fun to hang out with to something much deeper. She is not only seeking present happiness but future stable happiness and the happiness of her unborn children. If she doesn't want children the question will be more along the lines of do we have the same goals or are we going in the same direction in life?

Now, don't panic. A woman considering your fatherly factor question does not necessarily want to have children immediately, she just simply wants the commitment from you that it will happen in the future. If you do not provide this level of commitment she will feel very insecure in the relationship and will begin to seek a new partner who is not afraid of commitment and scores high in this regard.

How long is too long to wait? According to a survey, after three years she will begin to drop very obvious hints and after to four to five years the relationship is heading on a negative trajectory. The result will be that she will either dump you or ask you to ask her to commit.

Again in you are in a relationship for over four years and you are not considering marriage this is a strong indicator that you are not 100% satisfied with this woman and that you secretly think you can and will do better in the future. This current relationship is convenient at the moment and as a man you are not chained to a biological clock.

If you are afraid of rejection and that she might say no, there are a few methods that you can employ to help you overcome this fear.

For example if you walk into Starbucks, place and order and when the cashier requests payment, ask for a discount, of course she will say no to this question. You will pay the full price and nothing will have changed. If you do this a number of times you will begin to become immune to rejection.

Of course, having a Starbucks cashier deny your request for a discount isn't quite the same as the woman of your dreams shooting you request for her hand in marriage down, but these methods will give you the courage and confidence to ask in the first place. Your biggest fear should be that she gets frustrated and leaves you before you took the opportunity to simply ask.

35. Is There an Echo in Here?

Finding a creative way to propose is half the challenge, and you might be tempted to look around for inspiration. There is nothing wrong with doing so, but be careful where you source your ideas.

One of the men I interviewed, Jim, told me a story of how an all too familiar proposal went totally wrong. Jim's older brother, Mason, had proposed to his girlfriend, Terri, in one of the coolest ways. Wanting to really give Terri a proposal that would wow her, Mason arranged a skydiving trip, which was something Terri had always wanted to do.

After jumping out of the plane, a surprised Terri was soon met with a large banner on the field that read, "Will You Marry me?" As her skydiving partner brought her in closer to the landing spot, Terri spotted Mason at the foot of the sign waiting with the ring.

Jim loved this proposal so much that he copied it to a tee when it came time to propose to his girlfriend, Sarah. Sarah absolutely loved it, until she met Mason and Terri for the first time at Christmas and realized they had a lot in common. Yep, they swapped engagement stories and let's just say Sarah was not very pleased.

Every girl wants to feel like you put in the time to think through what she might like or dislike, and cater your proposal to her specific taste. She doesn't want someone else's proposal, she wants her own.

36. Liquid Courage

While some men are as cool as a cucumber on one of the biggest days of their lives, others are not so lucky. It's understandable and completely normal to feel nervous and anxious before popping the question. Some guys deal with the uneasiness by turning to liquid courage or other substances for a boost of confidence.

This is a terribly bad idea, which will more than likely come back to bite you when everything is said and done. One drink is fine, as this will calm you without damaging your ability to think clearly and maintain balance. It's easy to fall into the trap of just wanting one more but employ restraint; there will be plenty of champagne to follow afterwards.

Too much alcohol will lead you to forget some of you lines, slur your words or fumble with the ring. She will want you to look your best, so having a clear head and being fresh faced fresh is the path to follow.

Additionally, hopefully your proposal will be documented. Most people who have had a few drinks look terrible in photographs—red, sleepy or glazed over eyes, greasy hair, disheveled clothes and overly animated expressions. These photographs will be shared over and over again, they should not evoke feelings of shame or worst of all, not ring a bell. Sharp and sober is what you need to aim for not buzzed, blurry, or blacked out.

37. Worst Places to Propose

I know what you are thinking. I want to have a spectacular proposal in front of a giant crowd and await their applause and congratulations when she accepts my ring. We both enjoy football so where better then half time at the local stadium.
Wrong. If you are thinking this I strongly advise you in the most persuasive way I can to delete this idea from your head and try something else. This is not something she will find romantic. This is not how you propose to a lady.

Sports fans are the worst audience you could hope for. They paid good money to cheer their team and shout abusive profanity at the opposing team. The crowd will be male dominated and will likely have consumed a lot of alcohol. If you are going to intrude on their day out they will feel justified in intruding in on yours. They will not be quiet and they will not be polite.

Former class clowns, disenfranchised people, and trolls will rain down their opinions and lame attempts at making a funny from the stands zapping all hints of romance. In fact sports fan would find it much more entertaining if she rejected you rather than accept your ring and there will be a few who will do whatever they can to engineer this. For example, you won't be surprised to hear, "Don't do it!" "Save yourself!" or "Aw, come on!" from the more verbal and inebriated tools.

The Bedroom
Bedrooms have two purposes and two purposes only: sleeping and making love. Everything else should have something to do with those activities. Surprising her with breakfast in bed and a ring is not an ideal engagement. She will awake confused, groggy and sleepy, and she will likely not even register that you are about to pop the question. The logistics of you getting down on one knee are not clear and of course it will be nearly impossible to take a flattering photograph. The only exception to this is if you take her away on a beautiful vacation and your bedroom opens onto a spectacular view. But even then I would encourage more creativity.

The Office
Don't mix business with pleasure. She will not appreciate it if you decide to drop into the office and propose in front of all her colleagues and boss. Yes, you will definitely surprise her, but not in a good way. This will make her look unprofessional in front of her workmates. She could be very busy and not be able to spend the rest of the day with you. You need to consider what frame of mind you would like her to be in. She will be in work mode, stressed, busy and trying to appear formal and professional, when ideally for a

proposal she should be relaxed, well rested and in a happy mood. This is the prime mindset you desire for your best chance at an enthusiastic "Yes!"

I can't name every single place that might lend itself to a crappy proposal, but generally a good rule of thumb is to choose a setting that allows for an escape route. Take into consideration how awkward it would be in the event your girlfriend doesn't give you the answer you're hoping for. Any setting that doesn't make for an easy exit should be reconsidered.

Take, for example, proposing on a boat in the middle of the water or on an airplane. Would you want to row all the way back to shore in silence and tension so thick you could cut it with a knife? What about enduring another three hours of an airplane ride staring out the window while the woman who has just ripped your heart to shreds sits less than one feet away, while everyone surrounding you looks on at you with pity.

38. The Interweb

Have you heard about the man who tweeted "Will you marry me" to his girlfriend, or the football player who mailed a $75,000 ring to his girlfriend, only to be rejected?

What do these two Romeo's have in common? They both violated one of the first rules of proposing. I almost didn't think to include this in the book, because it should just be common sense that proposing over the Internet, telephone, text, and any other means besides in person is a huge no-no. Unfortunately, given the amount of men who have thought it was a good idea to try and pull off a virtual proposal, it appears it needs to be explicitly said.

A cardinal rule of proposing, that most men know better than to break, is to always propose live and in the flesh if you don't want your girlfriend to be eternally bummed about the day she got engaged, or increase the chances of her saying no. In fact, some guys go this route because they are very uncertain about being shot down and want to lessen the blow if a rejection is forthcoming, or they hope the pressure of proposing on the Internet where an online community is bearing witness (Twitter and Facebook, for example), will pressure a woman into saying yes.

There are so many things wrong with that line of thinking that I'm not sure where to start. First, if you are so scared that your girlfriend is going to shoot you down that you try to propose in a way that makes it easier for her to say no, or for you to hear a no, you probably shouldn't be asking in the first place. That's because she has more than likely given you reasons to be so insecure, or you haven't broached the topic with her beforehand.

If it's the former, you need to work on your relationship a bit more before contemplating marriage. If it's the latter, as discussed in an earlier section, another cardinal rule of proposing is to know that she is open and ready for marriage, particularly to you.

Secondly, if a woman says yes to supplicate you or spare herself embarrassment from the video going viral or people booing her if she doesn't give the expected answer, but knows in her heart she will turn you down privately later, you won't be any better off. In fact, you'll just have to then deal with and explain to confused family, friends, and well-wishers that you're not actually engaged or go into hiding to avoid being reminded every two seconds of the fact. You might even find yourself feeling jaded, and this might affect your future enthusiasm about proposing to another woman who may gladly want to be your wife.

Sure, technology makes everything easier, faster and more efficient, and has changed the way we do business and communicate. However, a marriage proposal should be sentimental and personal. This is simply one area of life that does not need to be replaced with computers.

Perhaps distance is a factor in your relationship, and the Internet, phone, computer, and text messages have played some significant role in its development. If that is the case, you could feel free to utilize the internet or technology in the proposal process, like maybe making her think she's talking to you on Skype, only to pop out and surprise her in real life. You then proceed to do the asking face to face.

Besides the impersonal factor, something about emails and text message doesn't do a very good job of conveying emotions. Things get lost in translation, jokes fall flat, etc. Even with phone calls where she may be able to hear your voice, she still can't see your expression, observe and commit to memory your body language, or see the emotion overtake you as you deliver your speech.

Furthermore, most women delight in the anxious anticipation before and bliss following a proposal, where she gets to exclaim "yes!" and jump into her man's arms, admire her engagement ring and have it slipped on to her finger, and even cry tears of joy on her guy's shoulder. If you are not present, she won't be able to adequately express her emotions towards you either.

For example, no hugs and kisses, no looking into each other's eyes, and no celebrating together afterwards. No image for her to hold on to in her mind for the remainder of her life, besides a telephone and Internet screen. You must realize how much you rob her of what should be one of the greatest experiences of her life. It's also worth adding, that you rob yourself of these gems as well.

This next reason for hesitation might not apply so much for snail mail, text messages, or emails, but the possibility of your Internet proposal going viral is very real for social media sites and videos (e.g. Google hangouts). If she says no, you can pretty much guarantee that it is going to go viral and you are going to look and feel like a complete idiot. Interestingly enough, even if she says yes and it goes viral, this can be a negative experience as well. Unfortunately, because of the anonymity of comment posting, your proposal could be the target of hundreds of naysayers making negative comments about nearly everything under the sun you can think of.

Another reason to abort any plan you may have had about digitally proposing being okay is that it is not the least bit romantic. Quite the contrary, it's cold and unreal. It is called virtual reality after all. Do you really want the woman you love hunching over her keyboard and peering at a computer screen when you claim you love her so much you want to be by her side forever and always. If you can't even make it to her side for the proposal, it doesn't come across as being very genuine and sincere.

Usually, I like to cover all the bases and try to find exceptions to the rule, and the only exception to the rule is not really an exception at all. It's more of a clarification. If you feel compelled to involve the Internet and social media in the way you choose to propose, you are free to do so, as long as somewhere along the line, you physically show up and pop the question.

As for exceptions to the rule for being completely missing in action, I'm sorry to tell you, but there are none. If you're in a long distance relationship, you wait until you can get in a plane or on a boat; or do whatever it takes for you to be there. Yes, you are going to share the rest of your life together but this is by far, the most important time to share together.

39. Why So Serious?

A proposal itself only takes a few minutes, it's what happens before and after that's so revealing and makes up the overall experience. Enjoy every single bit of it, because making a big to do about nothing or having a negative reaction to the unexpected mishaps that may occur, can completely affect your girlfriend's own enjoyment of the occasion.

Don't get me wrong, I'm not for a second saying you shouldn't take your marriage proposal seriously. After all, I've dedicated tons of hours researching, writing, and editing an entire book to help you deliver a darn-near pitch perfect proposal. I'm one of the biggest advocates for putting your all into this moment for your girlfriend and yourself.

What I am saying is that you should not take yourself or mishaps too seriously. Nobody enjoys being around people who have a poor sense of humor or intense energy. People like this can't relax, go with the flow, or let insignificant things go. Being laser focused on everything going right is akin to missing the forest for the trees. In other words, you are not looking at the big picture.

Don't forget what you're doing here. It's not the SATs and you won't automatically get a 'no' if there's a mishap. It's okay if everything doesn't turn out perfectly so lighten up. As long as the overall experience is fun, romantic and enjoyable, as opposed to rigid and stuffy, and she can see the effort you put in, you should be golden.

What ruins the happy atmosphere and enjoyable nature of the proposal is a sulky bloke, who insists on letting his disappointment and frustration be known either verbally or through negative body language. Particularly noteworthy are those guys who let a single moment affect their entire mood for the night. In many instances, she would have never known what was meant to happen if you hadn't bitched and moaned about that particular thing not going right.

Planning the proposal to the nth degree and not allowing for leeway isn't the best approach. As long as you've put in the work to organize and prepare, don't dwell on the things that are out of your control.

Besides, if you've read through the book and taken my advice, you'll have a backup plan if things get too out of hand.

Here's what you can control: your attitude, your focus—which should be your girlfriend—and doing everything you can to make the moment special and lighthearted for her.

Take this message into your marriage as well. The couples that can laugh at and with each other get this and are always the happiest. The ones who can't may have a seemingly great proposal story, but with the fun, warmth, and joy stripped out, will still be left lacking.

For example, one guy I interviewed for the book proposed to his girlfriend on a gondola ride. He had planned a number of activities throughout the day and everything thus far had gone swimmingly. Finally, the moment was upon him to propose.

However, as a self-described 'husky guy', finding his balance on one knee proved to be more difficult than he had imagined. For a solid half-minute, he slipped and rocked the boat before stabilizing himself while his girlfriend, laughing and giddy, looked on. It was like a comedy skit straight out of SNL.

Sure, he could have been pissed at himself for ruining the romantic atmosphere he had planned, but instead he laughed right along with his girlfriend. She said 'Yes' before he even got the words out.

Look, if you've paid for a service and the service and someone screwed up, heads can roll after the proposal is over, when your girlfriend isn't around to witness your tongue-lashing and get upset herself. If it's no one else's fault in particular, or you blame yourself for being absentminded, just let it go. Don't beat yourself up unnecessarily.

The same goes for rejections. Sure, it's a bummer if you are turned down, but don't go kicking yourself over it. Not all marriage rejects mean the end of a relationship. There have been countless men who have been turned down for various reasons ranging from asking too early to the woman not being ready, only to continue dating and get married later on.

Section VII - No Regrets

40. Wrong Intentions

People get engaged every day, some for the right reasons and others for the wrong ones. I don't mean to be the bearer of bad news, but not every proposal will lead to marriage, nor should it; it's just reality. The bad news is, since men are the ones who are expected to purchase a ring, and plan and pay for the proposal, if for whatever reason an engagement falls through, a man stands more to lose than the woman.

For example, take the engagement ring. When you offer an engagement ring as a gift, she gets to keep it if you don't happen to work out. This is especially true if you elect to propose on her birthday, Valentine's day or some other holiday where gift giving in commonplace. In some states, the person who gets to keep or take back the ring depends upon whoever calls off the engagement. However, if she has the ring already in her possession, and you no longer have access to her house, how easy do you think it will be to convince her to give the ring back to you?

This book was written with the goal of being the definitive source on the common mistakes most men make as it relates to proposing, and unfortunately, this blunder tops the list. It's also the least talked about mistake because it's automatically assumed that guys have already done a lot of thinking before making the serious decision to propose, but that's not always the case.

It has been my experience that a lot of men don't necessarily put as much thought into why and if they should be proposing in the first place. They think the proposal does not require the same amount of commitment as the wedding, and as such isn't as much of a big deal. I want to cover why you should, and more importantly what you should be considering, before you take an action you may come to deeply regret not only financially, but also emotionally.

For starters, you want to make sure you have decided to ask and marry the woman you are not only sure you love, but are compatible with and want to spend the rest of your life with. The last line is key. There are plenty of women that you could potentially fall in love with, but is this the woman that you cannot live without? If you cannot answer those questions decidedly, you might want to postpone any proposal plans you have ASAP.

Be honest with yourself when you contemplate exactly what your intentions are. If your intentions are outside of the scope of the above paragraph, and you propose anyway, you may come to regret that you didn't take the time to really assess them or heed my advice before entering into such a huge decision and contract. By the way, a marriage proposal is an orally binding contract.

Don't believe me? Ask Mr. Gibbs and Ms. Shell. Ms. Shell, who left her $80k per year job in Florida to move in with Mr. Gibbs, decided to sue Mr. Gibbs after he called off the wedding. A jury in Georgia awarded Ms. Shell $150k for the financial detriment she incurred relying on Mr. Gibbs' marriage proposal. She even got to keep the engagement ring.

I understand that not all men are as introspective as they should be, meaning they won't consciously realize they are proposing with the unhealthiest intentions. The result is a lot of people get hurt in the process when they do get real with themselves too little too late. If you really care for the person you are dating, don't lead them on or raise their hopes because you don't think proposing is a 'big deal'.

I've laid out some examples of what the wrong intentions and conditions are for you to propose so that you can reflect and more readily be able to answer if this is indeed the step you want to take.

You Want a Maid/Housewife

Sorry to break it to you, but this is not the 1950's. If the only reason you are proposing to your girlfriend is because you want a live-in maid and housewife, and you think it will be her duty once she gets married, you're in for a shock. It is rare to find a woman who wants to take on the old time traditional role of "wife" that used to come with expectations of minding the house and cooking dinner every night.

Even if she gives you the impression that she would be the 'perfect' housewife, what happens if a few months or years down the line she decides she doesn't want to do that anymore? Will that be a basis for the marriage to end? Marriage should not be transactional, or about an exchange of this for that.

You Want to Convince her to Do Something
Proposing to your girlfriend to get her to do something you want her to do, like getting her to move, allowing you to move in, or be physically intimate, is not only selfish it's morally wrong. It's called manipulation, not love, and nobody likes to be manipulated or used. What happens when you get your way, or you propose and she still doesn't budge?

Case of the Ex
Crazily enough, some men decide to pop the question to their current flame because an ex of theirs has recently gotten engaged or hitched, and they feel the need to play catch-up. Meanwhile, their poor fiancé is none the wiser that she is being played for a fool.

Some guys don't even realize their underlying motivation and just act impulsively on their hurt feelings, thinking proposing will make them feel better. It may do just that, but it's only temporary.

If you are still in love or pining for your ex, the last thing you need to do is be making a commitment to another woman. The heart needs time to heal, and dragging someone else into your life so that they can be a replacement before you are ready to really commit to them is generally an all around terrible idea.

You are Having a Baby
It's not my job to preach about the moral implications of proposing and marrying because you are having a child. Some people's religion pressure men or dictate that he has no other choice, and then there are the opinions of friends and family that oftentimes factor in to his decision. However, in my opinion, the most important thing for a child to have a happy life are loving parents that can work together as a team and get along. Solely having a child does not automatically mean that you and your child's mother are meant to be together.

You Don't Want to be Lonely
Are all of your friends coupling up and inviting you to their weddings? Do you find yourself with less and less buddies to hang out with because they're with their wives and families, and are planning on proposing to your girlfriend so you won't be left out of the crowd?

Then, you might want to stop in your tracks and do some major introspection.

The above are only jumping off points. There are so many other irresponsible and terrible reasons that guys choose to propose, that I can't possibly think to cover them in this short book. That's why I urge you to take the opportunity to think deeply about the matter before you go potentially upsetting someone else's life.

You might even consider talking to someone you can trust, and who is wise about such matters. In other words, don't go asking advice from a friend or family member that makes terrible decision and hasn't been able to maintain a long-term marriage. Seek advice from someone who appears to have gotten it right. The alternative is to speak with a therapist, pastor/clergyman, or marriage counselor for their take.

41. Ready or Not

Along the lines of proposing with the wrong intentions, proposing without a timeline to marry or the hope to remain engaged forever is a disaster waiting to happen. Maybe you read the previous section and determined that you have no ulterior questionable motives, love your girlfriend, and you make a good couple. She wants a proposal, and perhaps has been letting this fact be known, so you want to propose to appease her.

The only problem is your objectives do not align. She can't wait to start planning the wedding of her dreams and you have absolutely no desire to plan or go through with a wedding in the foreseeable future, or if you do it'll be a long time coming. It's okay if the idea of taking the permanent step that is marriage doesn't appeal to you, after all it's a lot less trouble to break up than to divorce. However, while you may not mind being tied up in engagement limbo, your girlfriend will likely feel much different.

You may also not realize now, but after the excitement has died down a bit and your girlfriend has finished admiring her new piece of jewelry, one of the first questions she will ask is your timeline for actually getting hitched. "Don't have one", or "let's just enjoy being engaged before we start talking about that," you say? It won't be music to her ears at all, and despite all the other great stuff that has just occurred, it'll be those words that stick with her for the remainder of the night, potentially ruining the entire proposal.

It doesn't stop there. As soon as word starts to spread that you are engaged, not only will you be barraged with questions about how the proposal went down (which is likely to end with her pouting or questioning the sincerity of the moment), you'll also be met with tons of inquiries about when the big day is by your friends and family members. Each month that passes, the questions will become more incessant and she will become more humiliated and impatient by your lack of interest in setting a date.

That's because one of the inherent nature of engagements is that they are meant to be only temporary. A survey conducted by Wedding Paper Divas showed that the average length of an engagement is twelve to eighteen months. A woman will ideally want her man to say confidently a year to a year and a half, or even sooner when asked when he wants to set the date. Mention much longer, or dismiss the wedding entirely as being far, far into the future, basically indefinitely, and you probably would have been better off not proposing at all.

Be prepared for arguments and her to feel confused and hurt. Can you blame her? Since you have somewhat indicated that you want to marry her by proposing, how can you explain not wanting to pinpoint a date? On top of all this, she'll have no problem holding you accountable and voicing her displeasure at every turn. In her eyes, she'll be back at square one, dating a guy who isn't serious about marrying her, and contemplating if she is only wasting her time.

You see, most women view dating as an investment, a risky one at that. In her prime years, 20's and maybe early 30's, she will have a much easier time securing a husband and potential father to her children because men place a great amount of value on youth and beauty.

When she locates a man who she thinks is a potentially good mate, she realizes that she only has a limited amount of time to spend before calling it a wash. Every time a relationship with one guy doesn't work out, the opportunity cost is her diminishing youth and beauty and high quality male prospects, since these men tend to get taken off the market fairly early.

She has to start all over again, which takes additional time—a commodity that she does not have. So, she needs to be smart and suss out the man who is in it for the long haul, or cut her losses. This is what will occupy her thoughts if you are not prepared to start planning a wedding shortly after proposing.

Much like the period before you propose, the longer you take to set a wedding date, the higher the perception you will never marry her. Adding more fuel to the fire will be her friends and family, who she will undoubtedly confide in. They will also echo her fears and might advise her to not waste any more time on you. The common thought being if it shouldn't take more than a few years to know if you want to marry someone, it definitely shouldn't take an additional few years to tie the knot once you've proposed.

I say all of that to say, if your goal of proposing stops at getting engaged, don't make the mistake of proposing in the first place. Utilizing this strategy to buy yourself a few more years without having to take the last step towards ultimate commitment will upset and completely embarrass your girlfriend when she realizes this fact. Women are very intuitive, and the second she unearths your lack of a timeframe to marry, regardless of the spectacle you may have put on the perfect proposal, she will still feel insecure and unhappy.

The second lesson is, if your goal is to eventually marry the wonderful woman you are going through all the trouble to impress and amaze, have a timeframe for the wedding handy. Know that she will probably be expecting you to say about a year, so be ready to throw out those numbers and mean it. You should also ask what she thinks is a good time frame in exchange, to let her know you respect and value her input on the matter as well.

42. The Guessing Game

What good ever comes from hinting? When it comes to asking your girlfriend to marry you, there is none. Hinting is like teasing, and nobody likes a tease. What you're saying is, 'I have a really great secret, but I can't actually tell you what it is.' If that were the case, then why the heck would you mention having a secret in the first place? You're practically begging someone to guess what in the world you might be alluding to.

Except, no one actually enjoys playing the guessing game to uncover a secret. It's exhausting. What's even worse is when you have no intention of letting the guesser know if she is right or wrong, because you've implanted an idea in someone else's head and their curiosity won't allow them to simply forget about it.

Add women, any woman, to this equation, and it gets even worse. Whereas your buddies might think you're lame for hinting at wanting to tell them something and then keeping tight-lipped, they'll usually respect your right to keep your secrets to yourself and leave you alone. With women, you could only be so lucky.

I've heard of cases where a guy couldn't keep his mouth shut to his girlfriend, and she consequently pouted and badgered him to tell her until it escalated to an argument and he caved, completely ruining the surprise. Take note, the same can occur with your mother, her friends, and your female friends. They just won't let up until you deliver on the checks your mouth foolishly wrote.

Another negative consequence of hinting about your intentions, is if your girlfriend figures out what you're hinting at and starts having expectations, she'll be disappointed every single time she's wrong. Sure, you haven't promised her anything, so how can she be upset and disappointed that her imaginary story that she has told herself isn't accurate?

How To Propose Without Screwing It Up

The same way you're disappointed when reality doesn't match up to your expectations, which are usually predicated upon some outside factor. For example, if your boss hinted about your awesome job performance right before review period, you'd expect things to go well and maybe a raise or bonus.

Should that same boss turn around and fire you or rip you to shreds in his written evaluation, you'd be confused, upset, and left feeling as though you were played for a fool.

Think about it and you will come to realize how much sense I am making. A buddy of mine, we'll call him Jason, told me of his plans to take his girlfriend to Paris for New Year's. He's a pretty frugal guy, so when he mentioned he had gotten a suite and had all these plans for his trip and started mentioning how life changing the trip would be, we all naturally assumed he was going to propose.

When he got back and we eventually caught up, one of the first things I asked was about his big trip. He started telling me about all the places he saw and what great fun he had, but when no details on his proposal were forthcoming, I had to come right out and ask him. Imagine my surprise when he revealed there was none. I'm sure his poor girlfriend was just as shocked and confused as I was.

Some guys feel the need to drop hints to throw their girlfriend off his scent, gauge her reaction, or to make sure that his girlfriend won't make plans that could interfere with his and ruin all his hard work. For example, you want to make sure that she's available and not tied up with something else, especially if your proposal arrangements require a lot of monetary investment that you won't be entitled to get back if you fail to show up.

However, none of the above are good reasons to start hinting and can backfire quickly, especially if you have to change your plans for any reason. Throwing your girlfriend off your scent will only frustrate her, and gauging her reaction to the idea of your proposing is not how you want to find out if she's ready for marriage.

While it is smart to make sure she won't be tied up on the day you propose, you need not prep her in this open ended and leading manner. Simply come up with a fake excuse that cannot be open to interpretation or ask her outright what her plans are on a certain day, then have a fake excuse when she wants to know why you care.

For example, say your friend is having a party, your mother has invited you guys over for a BBQ, you've scored tickets to the concert of a band she enjoys, as opposed to "I have a huge surprise for you coming up sometime next week; it's going to be awesome. You're going to love it!"

In the first scenario, she should have no reason to question whether any of those things are true, and the idea that you may be proposing won't enter her mind. In the second scenario, who wouldn't want to know what you were talking about? She'll wonder and start activating her imagination to fill in the gaps you've left in her head. If it turns out you are just taking her to a concert, but she already has visions of some elaborate proposal occurring, she'll be upset.

If a woman is ready to be proposed to, any small thing from you can be misconstrued as a sign that you are going to pop the question. To prevent such stress from occurring in your relationship, oppress any urge to hint at the proposal, as well as engage her in the guessing game for any other event or activity in your lives. Otherwise, even if it is your intention to eventually ask for her hand, you may feel pressured to propose on her time schedule instead of yours.

If you don't want to ruin the secret and fear that planning anything might set off her bells, a good technique to use is to plan your proposal around another important date or special event for the two of you, e.g. - your anniversary, or your annual trip to the ski lodge.

43. Making Assumptions

Does she even want you to ask her to marry you? This is a question you will be asking yourself again and again. It's totally common and all men go through this. It's a very difficult answer to ascertain because you simply cannot ask her in any sort of direct manner because it's considered unromantic. Even though communication is great for a relationship, this is the exception to the rule.

Pay close attention as this is one of the most common mistakes a man makes when preparing a proposal. In their mission to find the answer to the elusive question, they either make it very obvious and blow the surprise for her, or make assumptions and risk being rebuffed.

Making it obvious is a terrible idea, because if it is done incorrectly a woman will expect a proposal soon and if you do not deliver, she will be mad and frustrated. Making assumptions is just as bad because if your assumptions are off, things can get pretty awkward. You may find the life expectancy of your relationships take a turn for the worst, when if only given a bit more time, the outcome could have been different.

So how can one tell if a woman is ready for the same level of commitment? Keep reading and I will tell you exactly what techniques you can use and what signs you should be on the lookout for.

More often than not, women will be ready for commitment before men. Even if you arrive to this same conclusion at the same time it will be up to you to understand her indirect way of communicating this with you.

Now, since a woman is very unlikely to ask you to marry her directly, often they will leave some hints. Sure, when I write them out here it may seem completely obvious. However, if you are in the mindset of everyday life these secret messages can go unnoticed even by the most sensitive of men.

I am going to explain to you the most common ways a woman encourages her man to commit to her.

If you are walking down the high street and come across a jewelry store, she will make an excuse to go inside or peek through the window. If she expects you to accompany her and if she is very interested in your opinion on the jewelry, even though she normally does this with her girlfriends, you can take this as a very large hint at her wanting marriage. Don't be surprised if she points out how pretty the rings are and tells you which one she fancies. It's her way of making sure you get the ring right. Smart girl.

Another hint she will drop will be overtly commenting on other people's weddings, even when they are unrelated to you. Look out for phrases including,

"Wow, that's beautiful, I would like something like that," or "Those are gorgeous, I want to use the same ones for my wedding,".

Have you talked about marriage? If neither of you has brought up the subject, it might be time to do so. Not sure how to go about broaching the subject? One great way to do it is to simply ask her.

"What qualities are you looking for in your husband" Her answer will be telling. If she is lists qualities that she normally compliments you on it is a very good sign. However, if she replies that she is more concerned with her career, having fun right now, and has not thought about it, you should hold your horses and maybe not shell out any cash for a down payment on that rock.

Women will hint heavily at marriage and it's your job to be sharp enough to spot the clues she leaves. You will have to become an expert at picking up on the subtle hints she will give. I totally get that you're not a mind reader, but most women expect you to possess this magical trait anyway, so I've listed some of the most common hints to look out for below. Note, if she is not hinting then maybe she is not ready.

List of hints:

She will remind you how many years you have been together.

She will talk about how happy her newlywed friends are.

She will want to watch films like *Four Weddings and a Funeral, Wedding Wars, The Proposal,* or *Bridesmaids,* etc.

It may seem strange to us guys when the women in our lives make random observations about things. "Wouldn't that make a lovely wedding dress?" "Wow, I didn't know it was so cheap to rent a horse drawn carriage!", "Did you know that flowers are cheaper if you buy them direct in bulk from the flower district?" or "I want a wedding dress just like that."

These remarks seemingly come out of nowhere and just hang in the air waiting for a response that we can't fathom. In reality though, these statements are subtle, and sometimes not so subtle, forays into matrimonial discussions. Almost anytime marriage comes up in a relationship, even in a joke, there are serious thoughts behind it.

Women excel at being indirect; it's mostly how they communicate. You have to realize the underlying message and make of it what you will. Crack the code to their secret language by looking out for the above clues, and you'll have the answer you seek.

44. Missing The Moment

A picture is worth a thousand words and this is a picture you will want to see over and over again in the future, so be sure to plan appropriately.

When it comes to capturing the moment, there are a few options you have at your disposal ranging from free to a few hundred dollars. We'll start with your free options, which is to enlist the help of a friend or family member to secretly video record or photograph you so as to get a genuine reaction that you can forever look back upon.

Alternatively, you can rig the space beforehand with a secret camera or two, otherwise known as spy cameras. After everything is said and done, take the footage and edit it together yourself in an editing program or contract the work out using many of the freelance websites available. I am particularly fond of fiverr.com, freelancer.com, oedesk.com, and elance.com.

You can opt to share it with select friends and family on Facebook, or create a private video on YouTube. Of course, if your fiancé agrees to it, you can make it public for the entire world to see. Just be aware, that unless you turn the comments off or manually monitor each comment, some trolls will come along with nothing nice to say.

If your budget allows, hire a professional photographer and videographer. It doesn't need to be any of the expensive professional who dub themselves as 'marriage proposal photographers/videographers', with promises of being extra discreet.

There are plenty of freelance photographers and videographers on craigslist.com capable of doing a great job. Either post an ad letting them know what you're looking for and requesting a bid, or troll through the countless ads placed on the site every day of photographers actively seeking jobs. Ask for samples of their portfolios, references and contract before making a decision or leaving a deposit.

Alternatively hit up photography or film students. Their schools usually have job boards that you can post on. As with the professionals, ask to see samples of their work.

45. The Wrong Answer

If you thought being unprepared for what could be one of the best moments of you and your girlfriend's life was bad (not planning something special or creative), being unprepared for one of the worst moments of your life trumps that.

The importance of speaking with your girlfriend about marriage, looking out for hints that she's ready, and that she wants you to ask her, cannot be stressed enough. Sometimes, for whatever reason, even if you think all signs were pointing to a "yes", you may find yourself faced with a "no", "I'm not ready", or a "let me think about it", instead.

Do you have any idea what you are going to do if you hear anything else besides a yes?

I personally know of two instances where men have gotten no's to their proposals. One couple continued to date and later married, while the other split up. It's worth thinking about.

46. $#!t or Get Off the Pot

Are you the last 'single' couple left standing in a sea of similar aged friends planning weddings and going on honeymoons? Is your mother bugging you about grandchildren, and is your girlfriend watching an unusual amount of WETV?

If you've answered yes to any or all of these questions, you may be at risk of proposing under pressure. It's hard to stand up against the heat from your parents, friends, and an ultimatum from your girlfriend about finally stepping up to the plate. Before you know it, you've bought a ring, proposed, and find yourself wanting to get out of dodge on your wedding day. Don't let it escalate that far.

When your girlfriend starts plunking down an ultimatum, the translation is that unless you're prepared to get dumped you must ask her to marry you, after months, years, or even a decade of waffling. Realize that she's probably had multiple long sessions with her girlfriends before coming to her decision, and feels like everyone thinks she's a fool for staying with you as long as she has. She's probably not bluffing; so don't test her unless breaking up is something you seriously want to do.

I'm not endorsing you cave to her demands either. The thing is, once you propose, if you have second thoughts or doubts you can't just erase it from her memory or do a take back, so make sure you're certain it's what *you* want to do, since you're the only person who can live your life and you won't stand a very good chance of getting your expensive investment back should you come to your senses later on.

Before you go doing something you might regret, it's reflecting time. Can you pinpoint your reason for hesitating, or why you've waited this long? Do you think marriages tend to ruin relationships and want to stick with the status quo? Are you afraid that should anything go wrong, you'll be taken to the cleaners, or are you just not sure she's the one for you?

With serious introspection, either with a good therapist, or wise and experienced friend or mentor, whatever reason you come up with should dictate whether you propose, or break up and let your girlfriend move on with her life. You see, while you may think she's being irrational and rocking the boat, it's quite rational to stand up and say, "I know what I want, and if you want something different, maybe we should go our separate ways". If marriage matters to her but doesn't matter to you, what the heck are you two doing together?

Usually, in situations where a man waits forever, holding out until the last second to propose to his girlfriend, there's something wrong with him or his girlfriend.

There's Something Wrong With You
This is pretty much the only instance where you should go through with the proposal, after adjusting your beliefs of course. If you've given it some thought and realize that you are compatible and happy with your girlfriend (she's the one), but maybe afraid to make the commitment because of past negative experiences, your parents' relationship or what you've been fed by the media or 'pick up artist (PUA)' websites, stop being a coward and do right by her.

There's Something Wrong With Her
Now for the hard part; you've thought about it, gone to your therapist for advice, and got a second opinion from your best friend. All signs point to her not being the one. Maybe you're not a good match, have different beliefs/morals, or don't get along all that well. It's not rare for couples to stay together out of convenience or because of time already invested. This is the time to do yourselves a favor and end it, not

settle or plough through with a proposal with divorce as a contingency plan.

Don't make one of the most common mistakes and let yourself be pressured into proposing. You're only setting yourself up for a lifetime of misery.

47. Cry Me a River

Every guy is not going to be the vision of stoicism when they propose, nor should they be. However, there is a big difference between getting nervous or choked up, and becoming a blabbering, sopping mess.

If it's one thing you don't want your woman thinking as you are about to say the words she has been waiting to hear, is "Ugh". If crying women turn men off, and it does, according to research from Israel's Weizmann Institute of Science, crying men don't fare well with women either. Remember Boehner?

Many women find men's tears unsexy, distasteful, unsettling and if it's overdone, like some guys are wont to do when proposing, it can really screw up the atmosphere. It's not right that a woman would react negatively to a guy breaking down and being overwhelmed by his emotions for her, but you have to deal with reality and not what should be. There are nuances when it comes to the laws of attraction.

Besides, imagine if you were in her shoes. How would you feel if you were faced with an uncontrollably crying woman? Uncomfortable, clueless about what to do or say or do to console her, wishing that the moment would pass as quickly as possible so that you could remove yourself from the situation?

Maybe you'd feel embarrassed if there were tons of people around witnessing her sobs and judging her as lacking enough emotional stability and strength to reign in her tears while out in public. You know what, those would all be very fair and human reactions.

If you don't want to be perceived as weak or turn off your bride-to-be, do yourself a favor and do all you can to prevent a waterworks show from occurring. I should stress, a few strategically released tears won't be enough to illicit the automatic recoil reaction as mentioned above, so don't be afraid to show any emotion at all, just keep it under control. If you are the very emotional type, here's how to tone it down temporarily.

Prescription Drugs
Take a page out of the bridal secrets book by going to your doctor and getting him to give you something very, very mild for anxiety, perhaps a .5 klonopin. Get used to taking before hand to see how you will react. For example, if you aren't used to taking a lot of medication, it may make you sleepy, or it may simply

help you calm down. You can get a pill cutter and cut it in half if it is too much.

Section VIII - Closing Statements

48. Don't Sprint A Marathon

It's not every day that you ask someone to marry you, right? So don't treat it as such. By nature, proposing is a very important event and should not be squeezed into a busy schedule—for example, you may not want to schedule it in between your mom's birthday and your dad's retirement party.

Women are mysterious creatures but they all have certain things in common. Happily, the proposal is one of them and this allows us men to look at it from a logical perspective, break it down into components, analyze and devise a plan of action.

The bed you make is the one you will sleep in. I know this is a cliché saying but it's on point when it comes to planning a proposal. It's very important to prepare her mentally in the coming days before the big event. If you get her into the right state of mind about how she thinks about you, you will reap the rewards and guarantee yourself the perfect engagement. Here is a list of activities that will get her eyes glossed over every time she see you and it's not as complicated as you think.

Do the grocery shopping for the week.
Clean the house from top to bottom
Wash the dishes every night
Take the dog for its walks
Bring breakfast in bed
Cook her dinner
Buy her dinner

By completing the above activities you are proving to her that you want to take care of her and will be a good, stable and responsible partner, and convey you respect her and are willing to get your hands dirty for her.

Now she only thinks wonderful things when she thinks of you. If you are doing the above tasks on a regular basis then fantastic— she already believes in you. But there's no harm to put your efforts into overdrive on the lead up to the big question.

If you ask the question when she is in this mindset she will say yes to you as you have reminded her of the amazing qualities you possess. She will also be more relaxed and less stressed, which is also hugely beneficial.

In the coming days after the proposal there are also some tasks and considerations that will make the foundation for the beginning of a wonderful marriage.

Plan a wonderful date to the opera or somewhere similar where she can get dress up and show off her new ring.

Send her flowers at work. This will be a nice surprise and will allow her to feel special in the office.

Edit the video or photographs of the proposal. The sooner you have these to share the better. This is a perfect opportunity to make an album book that you can keep forever.

If you follow all of the above guidelines you will be on the road to happiness. It sounds like a long list and a lot of work and that's because it is long and difficult, but this is the woman you love so doing these task for her will feel like a breeze more than an arduous chore. On the plus side if you continue to drown her with considerations and gifts she will repay you with interest, but I will leave that up to your imagination.

49. It's Not Over

The big day has arrived. You have waited and planned it for what seems like an eternity, and everything has gone off without a hitch. You didn't lose the ring, remembered to drop to one knee, recited your speech with the finesse and skill of a Shakespearean actor, and successfully manage to sweep your girlfriend off her feet as evidenced by her reverent and enthusiastic "Yes!"

Congratulations, my friend. The hard work and investment into this book has paid off one hundred fold. You can now join the ranks of the minority of men who have pulled off a proposal worthy of your girlfriend's genuine approval. That's great, now have you thought about what will happen next?

You should have kept on reading, because committing this mistake is less of something guys do, and more of something that most men fail to do. I'm not sure many things can tank your efforts as fast for giving your women the proposal of her dreams.

Think about it, you have just created the biggest climax of her life, don't ruin it by suggesting an early night in and a DVD. Ideally, you should try to pick a day where both of you do not have to get up early and report to work the following day. You will want to be able to sleep in and hold each other, relaxing without the stress of work.

Immediately after you have popped the question your girlfriend, now fiancé, would probably be more than delighted if you've planned to have some professional photographs taken. It doesn't have to be long; a fifteen-minute session should suffice. If you have followed the instructions so far you will have chosen a very photogenic backdrop for your pictures. Alternatively, if the backdrop isn't the greatest, ask your photographer for suggestions. They will guide you.

If hiring a professional photographer is slightly out of your price range or if you want it to be more intimate be sure to have a tripod and camera setup, do some previous test shots, and have the camera on the correct time delay settings. It's not sexy to be fumbling around with this stuff and it will ruin the moment and the atmosphere.

Make sure her phone is fully charged and that yours is fully charged too. She will want to tell the world and her mother about the great news.

It is very important that you participate on the news sharing too. You should be proud of this and to prove it by screaming it from the top of your lungs right along with her. Post it on Facebook, tweet a video, ring all your friends and family, but if you have a lot of shared friends it's best to leave that part to her.

Give some thought to the order of your calls. Phone your closest family and friends first. This is an amazing phone call to be able to make, rarely do people pick up the phone to share or hear really happy news. The feedback you will get from people will be truly amazing, especially when you share your story of the perfect marriage proposal. Note, after sharing the news with your closest friends is the time to post it to social media.

If the night is still young, the fun shouldn't be over yet. Make sure to have plans for a show or dinner at a fancy restaurant where you can enjoy a fantastic meal together as a newly engaged couple. You could also have pre-arranged for a few of your close friends and family to gather at a meeting point for an post-engagement celebration with food and drinks.

If you choose to do dinner alone, or would rather not organize a big party with all your friends and relatives, you could elect to take your new fiancé to a swanky hotel for the night.

50. Have a Back Up Plan

Do you have a Plan A, B and C? Well, you should. Generally, if the day that you decide to propose isn't going as planned it is best to abort and wait until a more suitable time or better circumstances. For example she cannot join you because she got called into work and she cannot say no, or if she has come down with a terrible cold and looks like death warmed over, don't force the issue. Remember she will be photographed and she will really want to look her best.

Always be sure to have a twenty-four hour rescheduling clause when booking a photographer or renting something extravagant, like a hot air balloon. If you mention this up front and explain that you will only do so in extreme circumstances they should be accommodating. Not all companies will issue a refund, which is understandable, and it should not be a problem in any case. It's better to lose the money than push on and have a crappy result.

No matter how meticulous you are with your planning lady luck will always play a part. Mother nature is a harsh mistress and she can cause havoc with engagements. It can rain in the middle of July or September so you need to be ready to readjust the dates at the last moment if a storm is brewing and you're proposing outdoors.

Try to come up with as many reasonable scenarios as you can think of—even if you two are the only people concerned. For example, you might ask yourself the following questions:

What'll need to change if your girlfriend's running late?
What if she doesn't feel like going where you suggested?
What if either of you get sick?
What if there's a government shutdown and the Statue of Liberty is closed?

Okay, maybe you can't predict the completely unpredictable instances, like a government shutdown. That's when, as anxious as you may be to get engaged, postponing your proposal can sometimes be your best option.